SACRED CIRCLES:
prehistoric stone circles of Wales

Sacred Circles:

prehistoric stone circles of Wales

Julian Heath

First published in 2010

© Julian Heath

© Llygad Gwalch 2010

ISBN: 978-1-84524-160-5

Cover design: Eirian Evans

Published by Llygad Gwalch,
Ysgubor Plas, Llwyndyrys,
Pwllheli, Gwynedd, Wales, LL53 6NG,

www.carreg-gwalch.com

For Georgia and Lawrence – the two terrors

Acknowledgements

Firstly, I must thank Myrddin ap Dafydd for commissioning this book, the writing of which allowed me to explore a fascinating aspect of life in prehistoric Wales and also took me to many parts of its magical countryside that I had not visited before. Secondly, I must express my gratitude to Graham Tickner who very helpfully provided several photographs of sites that I was unable to visit. Thanks also go to Dr Peter Hodges who provided photographs of Bedd Arthur and Saith Maen, and to The Royal Commission on Ancient and Historical Monuments in Wales, who kindly supplied the picture of the Nant Tarw circle. Lastly, I must say a big thank you to Jen Llywelyn for providing encouragement when things didn't go to plan and for editing and improving the text.

Sacred Circles:

Contents

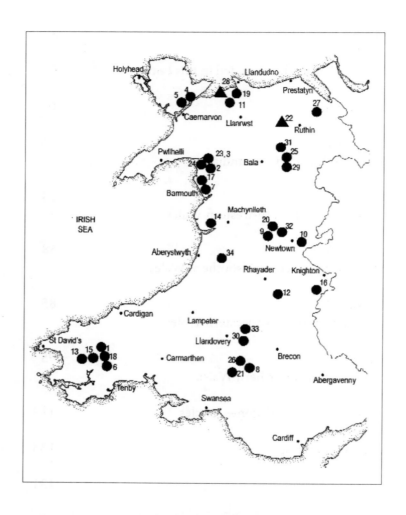

Approximate location of circles included in book

List of stone circles included in this book
(Numbers before circles correspond to numbers on map opposite)

Welsh name	English translation
(1) Bedd Arthur	'Arthur's grave'
(2) Bedd Gorfal	'Gorfal's grave'
(3) Bryn Cader Faner	'outlook post on the hill'
(4) Bryn Celli Ddu	'hill of the dark hazel grove'
(5) Bryn Gwyn	'white hill'
(6) Buarth Arthur/Meini Gwŷr	'Arthur's enclosure/'soldiers' stones'
(7) Cerrig Arthur	'Arthur's stones'
(8) Cerrig Duon	'black stones'
(9) Cerrig Gaerau	'the stones of the hill forts'
(10) Ceri Hill	
(11) Cerrig Pryfaid	'the stone of the flies'
(12) Crugiau Bach	'little hillocks'
(13) Dyffryn Syfynwy	
(14) Eglwys Gwyddelod	'church of the Irishman'
(15) Eithbedd	'gorse grave' (possibly)
(16) Four Stones	
(17) Ffridd Newydd	'new pasture'
(18) Gors Fawr	'great marsh'
(19) Hafodty	'summer home'
(20) Lled-Croen-yr-Ych	'the width of the ox-hide'
(21) Llorfa	
(22) Llyn Brenig Group	
Llyn Brenig 44	
Llyn Brenig 51	
Llyn Brenig 8	
(23) Llyn Eiddew Bach	'little ivy lake'
(24) Moel Goedog West and East	'Goedog hill'
(25) Moel-Tŷ-Uchaf	'the hill of Tŷ Uchaf'
(26) Nant Tarw	'the bull-brook'
(27) Penbedw	'the edge/head of the birch grove'
(28) Penmaenmawr Group	
Circle 278	
Monument 275	
Monument 280	
Red Farm	
Y Meini Hirion/Druids' Circle	
(29) Rhos-y-Beddau	'moor of the graves'
(30) Trecastle Mountain	
(31) Tyfos Uchaf	uncertain – could be 'Tŷ Ffos' – 'the house on the ditch'; 'uchaf' means 'higher'
(32) Y Capel	'the chapel'
(33) Ynys Hir	'long island'
(34) Ysbyty Cynfyn	'Cynfyn's hospice'

Introduction

Many thousands of years passed before the country of Wales emerged into written history. Before this time, in the prehistoric period, the lives and deeds of people are unknown and they remain forever nameless. Nevertheless, the abundant archaeological evidence that survives in the Welsh countryside ensures that although these people may be long gone, they are not forgotten. From the handaxes left behind by Neanderthals in Pontnewydd Cave (Denbighshire), to magnificent hillforts of the Iron Age, such as Tre'r Ceiri (Llŷn, Gwynedd), we are reminded of some 225,000 years of prehistoric life.

The countless artefacts, sites and monuments from this time have provided us with a wealth of valuable information and new discoveries continue to enhance our understanding of prehistoric Wales. However, for me at least, the most fascinating periods in Welsh prehistory are the Neolithic, Copper and Bronze Ages. It was during the Neolithic that agriculture was introduced into Britain and people began to settle in permanent farming villages, whilst in the Copper and Bronze Ages the secrets of metalworking were discovered. The combination of these two activities provided a potent force for change and it is beyond doubt that, ultimately, the establishment of agriculture and metalworking had a profound impact on the development of modern civilisation.

In addition to this powerful legacy, the communities who lived during these times have also left us with a huge and diverse collection of monuments which continue to cast their enigmatic spell on those who feel compelled to look backwards into our ancient past. Although we are groping in the dark somewhat when it comes to the realities of prehistoric life, evidence found at these monuments casts a little light into this darkness, and allows us to edge closer to the people of a long-vanished world.

Among the most intriguing of these monuments are the stone circles that were erected throughout the British Isles; it is evident from excavations undertaken at various examples that the tradition of stone circle building had a lengthy history. The first examples were raised in the Late Neolithic, perhaps as early as 3200 BC, and it seems that they continued to be built for some 2000 years, with the last stragglers probably making their final appearance in the Middle Bronze Age about 1200 BC.

Of course, the most famous stone circle in the British Isles is the awe-inspiring Stonehenge, but this atypical example is just one of hundreds still surviving in the landscape. In fact, in *Prehistoric Stone Circles*, Aubrey Burl tells us that more than 1300 stone circles in varying states of preservation have been recorded in a recent survey, and he plausibly suggests that originally, there may once have been as many as 2000 stone circles in the British Isles. Although none of these circles can match the grandeur of the mighty megalithic ring that sits on Salisbury Plain, they are nevertheless just as relevant as their celebrated counterpart.

Wales does not have a particularly large number of stone circles (some 5% of the British total) but many of these are well worth visiting. This book is intended as an introduction and guide to thirty-four of these compelling places. We will also briefly consider what, if anything, the stone circles of Wales reveal about their original purpose and whether they can tell us anything about the people who erected them in lonely and beautiful corners of the Welsh countryside. It should also be pointed out that although all the main sites and many of Wales' stone circles are included in this book, it is not a comprehensive overview of these monuments, and the others are well worth visiting too. Those readers wishing for a complete inventory of stone circles in Wales are directed to the websites listed at the back of the book.

Personal experience of visiting many prehistoric monuments in Wales has taught me that such visits are not always as straightforward as I anticipated when I looked on the map. With this in mind, I have included a gazetteer for those readers who intend to visit the stone circles featured in this book. I have also included additional details of other archaeological sites of interest that can be found near the circles. However, these details are by no means exhaustive and only really scratch the surface of the countless prehistoric sites that can be found in the regions covered. The maps needed for site visits belong to the excellent Ordnance Survey *Landranger* series and are available in good bookshops and camping shops, as are the Ordnance Survey *Explorer* maps, which some readers may prefer to use.

Julian Heath
May 2010

Remember ...

Before you go, tell someone where you're going.

Even if you take a mobile phone with you, there might not be good reception all the way. (But please, keep it switched off, or in 'silent' mode!)

Read the walk description carefully before leaving, and make sure you're wearing the right footwear; it's always a good idea to take waterproofs in a rucksack – in Wales, the weather can change very suddenly.

THE COUNTRY CODE
- Guard against any risk of fire.
- Keep to public rights of way when crossing farmland.
- Avoid causing any damage to walls, fences and hedges.
- Leave farm gates as you find them.
- Keep dogs under control and on leads in the presence of livestock.
- Leave machinery, farm animals and crops alone.
- Take care not to pollute water.
- Carry your litter home with you.
- Protect all wildlife, plants and trees.
- Avoid making any unnecessary noise.
- Drive carefully on country roads.
- Enjoy and respect the countryside.

Chapter 1

Stone Circles: a Brief Examination

The hundreds of prehistoric stone circles that can be found scattered throughout the British Isles undoubtedly rank among the most evocative memorials to the remote and mysterious time in which they were erected. Since the late 18th century, when antiquarians such as William Stukeley and Edward Lhuyd initiated their emergence from obscurity, stone circles have proved to be an enduring source of fascination, fuelling both academic and popular imaginations alike. It should also be pointed out that many stone circles of a much more recent date can be seen in the parks and open spaces of towns throughout Wales. Something must be said about these monuments, as they have some significance in respect of Wales' cultural heritage.

Iolo Morganwg and the Gorsedd Circles

These more recent circles were erected for the *Gorsedd* ('high seat') ceremony that forms an important part of the annual *Eisteddfod* – the national arts and music festival which has been a major force in the preservation of the Welsh language and culture. It is worth noting that the first Eisteddfod was held at Cardigan (*Aberteifi*) castle in 1176, by the famous Rhys ap Gruffudd (the Lord Rhys), one of medieval Wales' greatest leaders. In plan, the Gorsedd Circle consists of twelve stone pillars (unfortunately, replica (fibre-glass) stones are now used in the Gorsedd ceremonies), with a large, flat-topped central stone known as the *Maen Llog* ('the logan stone'), from where the

Archdruid leads the ceremony. Outside the circle, facing the *Maen Llog* at the east cardinal point, is the *Maen y Cyfamod* ('the stone of the covenant') where the Herald Bard stands. Behind the Maen y Cyfamod are the *Meini'r Porth* ('the portal stones', which give access to the inner circle), with the stone to the right pointing to sunrise on midsummer's day and the stone on the left orientated to the rising sun at midwinter. As we will see later, the orientation of these outer stones is paralleled in some of the prehistoric stone circles of Wales, although it is highly improbable that the Gorsedd ceremony reveals a long unbroken tradition stretching back into prehistory. Rather, it reveals the fertile imagination of one of the most fascinating and celebrated characters of Welsh history – Edward Williams or Iolo Morganwg ('Edward of Glamorgan') to give him his bardic name, by which he is more commonly known.

Iolo Morganwg (1747–1826) came from a humble background and was born in the village of Pennon in Glamorgan (*Morgannwg*). Like his father, he became a stonemason by trade, though from early on, he was interested in early Welsh literature and ancient Welsh culture in general. However, although he collected and published a number of genuine works of early Medieval Welsh literature (e.g. *Hanes Taliesin*), he was also a great forger and among his many forgeries were poems attributed to the great fourteenth-century poet, Dafydd ap Gwilym, and a book said to have been written by Saint Cadog. Iolo also claimed to have access to a genuine manuscript (*Barddas* – said to be a sixteenth-century work by one Llywelyn Siôn) which recorded the traditions of the druids and bards from before the time of the Romans, and he claimed to have found a record and plan of the prehistoric Gorsedd circle used by the Iron Age druids.

In 1792, the first 'modern' Gorsedd ceremony was held

on Primrose Hill in London. It was Iolo Morganwg himself who led an assembly of important Welsh 'exiles', laying out a circle of pebbles, within which a druidic ceremony was held. Although this first Gorsedd attracted some publicity, it very nearly became a curious footnote in Welsh history because Iolo's staunch support of the French Revolutionaries was not looked upon favourably in Wales. However, Iolo was undeterred and as Iorwerth C. Peate has said, 'Iolo's next step to save his movement revealed his genius [and he] grafted his druidic movement on to the eisteddfod'. On the Saturday following the Eistedfodd held by the Cambrian Society of Dyfed in 1819, Iolo held his first Welsh Gorsedd at the Ivy Bush Hotel in Carmarthen (*Caerfyrddin*). The consequence of this clever move was that by the late nineteenth century, the Gorsedd had become an integral part of the annual Eisteddfod in Wales; furthermore, the Gorsedd circles now resembled their prehistoric counterparts, with large standing stones used in their construction.

Many modern scholars agree that like many of his other claims, those Iolo made regarding the prehistoric authenticity of the Gorsedd ceremony are highly spurious to say the least, and, in fact, that he invented it. It is worth mentioning, though, that there are references to Gorsedds in ancient Welsh literature such as the famous *Mabinogion*. However, in these early works, they are described as lofty mounds which were used as judicial meeting places. Nevertheless, the Gorsedd circle and its attendant ceremony and rituals invented by Iolo Morganwg in the late eighteenth century are in their own way just as important, as they have certainly played their part in the preservation of a strong and independent Welsh identity.

The Function of the Prehistoric Stone Circles

It is hardly surprising that every year many people are drawn to visit the stone circles of the British Isles as they are often quiet and contemplative places surrounded by stunning tracts of countryside. Also, these silent rings of stone are deeply mysterious monuments that leave the modern visitor yearning to know what motives lay behind their construction and what took place within their now weathered and lichen-covered stones. Such concerns may seem futile when it is considered that their non-literate builders are firmly consigned to the dim recesses of prehistory. However, all is not lost, as the stone circle builders left behind them tantalising archaeological clues that go some way to helping us uncover the answer to these circular riddles of stone.

Places for the Dead

The firmest statement that we can make in regard to the function of stone circles is that some were used as cemeteries. Several examples have yielded human burials in their interiors – usually in the form of cremations. It seems, though, that not all cremations found within stone circles represent successive burials made in a family or group cemetery, as they are too small and incomplete in this respect. Therefore, they appear to represent deposits or offerings connected with the unknown rites that took place within the confines of the circles. The most notable example of a stone circle being used as a burial place has to be Stonehenge, with archaeological evidence discovered during various excavations in the twentieth and twenty-first centuries revealing that its interior was used as a cremation cemetery between *c.*3000–2400 BC. It is possible that some of these burials represent the members of a prehistoric dynasty whose origins lay in Europe, but who settled in

Wales and who later established themselves (either by force or by more subtle methods of coercion) as a powerful elite that may even have held sway in the Stonehenge region for around 500 years.

An intriguing idea proposed by Mike Parker Pearson and the Madagascan archaeologist, Ramilisonina, is that Stonehenge was built primarily as a place for the spirits of the dead or the ancestors. They suggest that although at some point the living will undoubtedly have visited Stonehenge to perform ceremonies and rituals connected with the dead, for the most part Stonehenge was left alone as a dwelling place for the ancestors. Parker Pearson and Ramilisonina draw on evidence from small-scale societies in Madagascar, where standing stones are closely linked to the honouring of the ancestors. Similar beliefs were recorded among tribal peoples in Indonesia by the early twentieth-century anthropologist W. J. Perry, who found that standing stones were seen as the dwelling places of both remote ancestors and recently-deceased relatives. Some tribes believed that stones were also inhabited by guardian spirits, and in some cases these guardian stones could not be erected until they had been bathed in the blood of a human sacrifice. In a similar gruesome vein, the heads of enemy slain were left at the feet of some stones before being removed for display in nearby huts. As we will see later, there are dark hints of sacrificial practices taking place at some of the Welsh stone circles.

The idea that stone circles were places for the dead that were little visited by the living, could be applied to many of the other less spectacular, but more typical, stone circles found throughout Britain. The generally scanty evidence found in their interiors lend some support to this theory. However, as the familiar archaeological saying has it, 'absence of evidence is not evidence of absence'. It is quite possible – if not probable – that stone circles were places with strong links to the ancestors, but the living could still have frequently visited stone circles to perform religious rituals and ceremonies that would leave no discernable traces in the archaeological record.

Dancing Places?

One intriguing possibility to consider in regard to the rituals and ceremonies that took place within stone circles is that some form of dancing played a significant part in these, particularly in the larger examples. This idea is lent some weight by the very shape of the stone circles themselves, as their interiors would lend themselves very well to dancing. There is also the fact that many British stone circles have folk-names and legends that can be firmly linked to dancing. For example, the 'Trippet' stones and the 'Merry Maidens' in Cornwall are said to be young girls who were turned into stone because they had the temerity to dance on the Sabbath. Similar tales are associated with many other British stone circles. Also in Cornwall, we have the circles known as 'the Blind Fiddler' and 'the Piper of Boleigh'. Much further north in Shetland, there is a circle known as 'the Limping Dance' while at the Stanton Drew circle in Somerset there is an avenue of stones known as 'the Fiddlers'. Of course, such folklore does not provide proof of prehistoric dancing at stone circles; nonetheless, the possibility remains that it contains echoes of the ancient practices that took place at these monuments.

Interestingly, ritual ring-dancing has been recorded among societies that would have shared some similarities with those who built the stone circles. The American Creek Indians, for example, celebrated the annual harvest by dancing around fires, before purifying themselves of their past sins in running water. Perhaps the most famous example of ritual ring-dancing among tribal peoples is the 'Ghost Dance' performed by the Indians of the Great Plains of North America. Sadly, this dance needed to be performed as an appeal to the ancestors to rid the land of European settlers, and to bring back the vast herds of buffalo that they had wiped out.

Examples of ritual ring-dancing at special times have also been recorded among more recent European societies, with maypole dancing a widespread and familiar occurrence. On the Isle of Man, there was a somewhat cruel but intriguing ritual which involved people dancing to music after they had killed and buried a wren at the Winter Solstice.

Science versus Symbolism

It is now widely recognised that many stone circles are aligned on astronomical events such as the sun rising at midsummer, or setting at midwinter. Exactly why prehistoric communities orientated their stone circles (and other monuments) on such events remains with their long-dead builders but for many years it has been, and continues to be, a contentious issue.

Although earlier archaeologists (e.g. Sir Norman Lockyer who was the first person to recognise that the passage of the Bryn Celli Ddu Neolithic tomb on Anglesey (*Ynys Môn*) was aligned on the rising midsummer sun) had shown interest in astronomical alignments at prehistoric monuments, it was not until the publication of Professor Gerald Hawkins' *Stonehenge Decoded* in 1965 that 'archaeoastronomy' really began to capture both academic and popular attention. Gerald Hawkins was an astronomer at Boston University in America and the underlying premise of his work was that Stonehenge had been designed as an observatory by highly skilled astronomer-priests, who used it as extremely sophisticated 'machine' for recording solar and lunar eclipses, the knowledge of which was passed on to succeeding generations.

Following Gerald Hawkins' highly controversial but very popular book was Alexander Thom's *Megalithic Sites in Britain* (1967), in which this highly energetic professor of engineering at Oxford University (who undoubtedly did much to further the subject of archaeoastronomy) identified what he felt were high precision solar and lunar alignments in many stone circles and other prehistoric monuments. Alexander Thom continued to pursue his passion for prehistoric astronomy well into his retirement and eventually, he came to believe that among the prehistoric communities of Britain, there were people who were observing and recording astronomical events in much the same way as modern astronomers do today.

However, the theories put forward by scholars such as Gerald Hawkins and Alexander Thom are now questioned by the majority of archaeologists. The current consensus is that because many astronomical alignments are low-precision or 'rough' they are thus more likely to be symbolic of ideas relating to the gods, death, ancestor worship and the like, rather than the existence of a 'megalithic science'. Nevertheless, while the evidence does point more strongly in the former direction, in some cases at least, prehistoric people in Britain do appear to have incorporated precise alignments into their ritual monuments, even though these sightlines to the sky probably had more do with ideology than intellectual enquiry.

Stone Circles and Geometry

Thanks to Alexander Thom's research, it is now widely accepted that many stone circles are actually not true circles, with many laid out in non-circular shapes, and we should look briefly at Alexander Thom's remarkable theories in regard to how these non-circular monuments were designed. Basically, he proposed that a prehistoric unit of measurement known as the 'Megalithic Yard' (equal to 0.829 m) existed in Britain and Brittany and that ultra-precise yardsticks (which were manufactured in a central 'depot' and sent out all over Britain) were used to lay out right-angled Pythagorean triangles which formed the templates for the stone settings. However, although it is evident that some level of skill and planning did go into the laying out of the non-circular (and circular) rings, it is generally felt that it is more likely that less sophisticated methods of measurement were used in their construction. In many documented stateless societies around the world, body measurements such as the foot, forearm, or body-yard were employed by the builders of both secular and ritual monuments. Of course, such ethnographic evidence cannot be taken as irrefutable proof that stone circle construction gangs did likewise, even though it does lend some credence to the idea.

Sacred Geography

One thing that is striking about the stone circles of Britain is that many are located in positions which afford wide-ranging views of the landscape, and often, they are ringed by distant hills and mountains which form natural arenas around them. Several British stone circles also appear to have been deliberately aligned on conspicuous hills and mountains. For example, as far back as 1892, A. L. Lewis had claimed that he knew of some one hundred stone circles that were aligned on prominent hills, while in 1926, Lily Chitty realised that three gaps in the Black Marsh stone circle in Shropshire were aligned on surrounding hills; she placed walking sticks against stones 19 and 20 and found that they exactly framed Corndon mountain in the distance.

It is unlikely that the repetition seen in the location of stone circles can simply be put down to coincidence, although exactly what it means, we can of course never know for sure. However, it does seem to indicate a prehistoric perception of the landscape that was very different from our own. Like us, prehistoric people surely appreciated the beauty and grandeur of the natural world, but they probably also viewed the landscape as a sacred and powerful place that was associated with supernatural forces. It is evident that such beliefs were, and are, very common amongst 'primitive' societies and often, prominent landscape features such as hills and mountains are associated with the creation of myths and tales. For example, the Zuni Indians of Arizona still continue to make a 100-mile-long pilgrimage to a site near Ribbon Falls in the Grand Canyon, where they believe the 'First People' emerged. Similarly, the Huichol Indians of Mexico trek some 300 miles to the Wirikuta Plateau, which is viewed as their mythical homeland.

It is also possible that some stone circles were actually symbolic representations of the landscape, as has been credibly suggested by the respected British archaeologist Richard Bradley, for circles such as Castlerigg in the Lake District and the Stones of Stenness and the Ring of Brodgar on Orkney. The likelihood is that it was not just the deities and spirits of the sky that were worshipped by the stone circle builders, but also those that dwelt within the landscape itself. Therefore, it is quite possible that they felt that it was important that a 'supernatural connection' was not only made between the circles and the sky, but also with the sacred geography that surrounded these monuments.

Trading Centres

Many archaeologists agree that it is likely that some of Britain's stone circles were also used as places to trade the characteristic stone axes that were used by Neolithic communities throughout Britain. In the Lake District, for instance, several of the major stone circles of this region seem to have been located close to the sites of stone axe factories and the routes that led to these factories. However, while many of the traded axes were undoubtedly used as tools and also as weapons of war, it should be remembered that archaeological evidence has revealed the existence of a widespread axe-cult in Neolithic Europe. For example, at one of the Llandegai 'henges' (circular earthworks usually featuring a circular earthwork and inner ditch – although Llandegai and a small number of other henges have outer ditches) near Bangor in north Wales, stone axes were deliberately buried within the monument. Another Welsh site revealing the ritual importance of Neolithic stone axes is at Perth Chwarau in Denbighshire, where a stone axe was buried in front of a cave that was used as Neolithic tomb. In the Somerset Levels, a beautiful jadeite axe that came from the Swiss or Italian Alps was deliberately deposited beneath the famous 'Sweet Track' – a wooden trackway (dated to 3807/6 BC) that gave Neolithic people access across an area of wet fenland. In County Sligo, another superb diorite axe was buried in the forecourt of one of the finely built court-cairns which are distinctive to Ireland. On the continent, at the site of Troldebjerg, Denmark, a stone axe with its cutting edge upwards was found buried in the hearth of a Neolithic longhouse, and similar finds have been made at Neolithic tombs in Brittany. Tiny perforated axes made from pretty, coloured stones have also been found in Neolithic contexts in Brittany and these probably represent amulets worn around the neck designed to protect their wearer from the nefarious intentions of both the dead and the living. It seems probable then, that some of the stones axes that were traded within the stone circles of Britain were destined for ritual deposition rather than practical usage. Perhaps prehistoric people deposited axes in stone circles and other monuments because they felt that they had to give thanks to, or to placate, the spirits or deities that were believed to dwell in the stone axe quarries which were often located on significant hills or peaks.

Alternatively, like the beautiful axe that was deposited beneath the Sweet Track, axes buried in the ground may also represent offerings to dark and dangerous deities who inhabited a frightening underworld. We may even have fascinating evidence of Neolithic people attempting to protect themselves from such deities at the remarkable flint mines of Grimes Graves in Norfolk. Here, in the early third millennium BC, Neolithic miners placed a chalk figurine of an obese, large-breasted woman (not unlike the 'Venus Figurines' associated with the much earlier Upper Palaeolithic period on the continent) on the floor of a deep shaft in the underground galleries. While it is possible that the miners were asking a powerful female goddess for help in finding abundant seams of good quality flint, it is equally possible that they were asking for protection from roof-falls and collapses, which could have been attributed to malevolent spirits of the underworld.

Archaeological discoveries confirm that this cult of the axe continued into the European Copper and Bronze Ages, though of course, now the axes were made from metal, rather than stone. Thousands of copper and bronze axes have been found at various ritual and funerary monuments from these periods; many sites also feature carvings of copper or bronze axes. One of the most famous examples of this practice comes from Stonehenge, where some of the huge sarsen stones are decorated with carvings of such axes – their splayed blades pointing to the sky, perhaps in supplication to the sun and moon, which were surely major deities in the prehistoric 'pantheon'.

Stone Circles and 'Celtic' alignments

It is also apparent that many stone circles in Britain feature alignments that point towards sunrise or sunset at times of the year that were ritually important to the famous Celts of the Iron Age (e.g. Beltane and Samhain, which have survived into our times as May Day and Hallowe'en), and which they celebrated by holding major festivals. Such alignments do not provide proof that similar festivals were held by those who built the stone circles or that the beginnings of a Celtic culture existed among them. However, they do suggest that we should not be too ready to discard the idea that the ritual beliefs and practices of the Iron Age had their roots amongst earlier prehistoric communities in Britain.

Overall, then, the evidence gleaned from stone circles indicates that although they were simple in form, they were complex monuments that functioned on several different levels and which enshrined the religious beliefs of their builders. We should perhaps also consider the possibility that British stone circles could be used for more prosaic, secular purposes on occasion. Some support for this idea may be provided by ethnographic evidence from Cameroon. Here, stone circles dating to the Iron Age are not only associated with the worship of ancestral spirits and with rites of purification and protection, but until recently, several were still being used as 'council chambers' and 'courts' where various tribal and familial matters were discussed and resolved.

It is perhaps worth saying that many of our familiar churches, in their hundreds of years, have been used for religious and secular ceremonies, market days, places of refuge, festivals, stabling for horses, and, more recently, as community centres, carpet warehouses, and domestic dwellings. In most churches there are burials of many kinds, at many dates, and many other memorials. Why should we expect stone circles not to have had a similar variety of uses?

Chapter 2

Stone circles of south-western Wales

Gors Fawr

North Pembrokeshire in south-western Wales is home to some of Britain's most stunning landscapes and this area also contains some of Britain's finest prehistoric monuments. Amongst these is the Gors Fawr stone circle, which is located on an atmospheric expanse of heathland that lies just below the Preseli Hills near the village of Mynachlog-ddu. Aubrey Burl has referred to this heathland as 'a peat-drenched and drab low-lying common', but a visit to the site on an early evening in August , when the cloud-flecked sky above the surrounding green of the rolling hills was a pure blue, left me with a different impression.

The local name for the circle is *Cylch y Trallwyn* (which translates as the rather mysterious 'circle of troubles'). Although the low stones of Gors Fawr are not particularly noticeable among the long tussocks and stubby bushes that cover the heathland, it is nevertheless a well preserved monument. The circle is about 22.5 metres in diameter and features sixteen weathered boulders of local origin, with at least eight of the stones being of the distinctive spotted dolerite that outcrops on the striking summit of nearby Carn Menyn. The stones of the circle rise slightly in height as they progress from north-west to south-east, with the lowest stone reaching about 0.5 metres and the tallest about 1 metre. This grading in height can also be observed in stone circles found on Dartmoor, and in particular, the Fernworthy circle, which closely parallels Gors Fawr, both

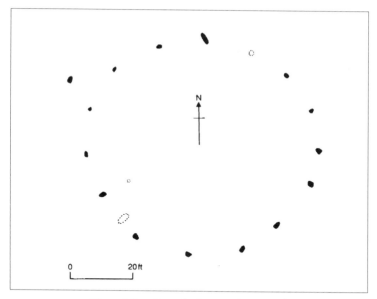

Plan of Gors Fawr (redrawn after Thom)

in the grading of its stones and in its diameter. Such similarities may indicate contacts between the two areas and such contact may even have involved the arrival of 'foreign' circle builders in the Preseli Hills or vice versa.

About 130 metres to the north-east of the circle are a pair of large standing stones, which both measure nearly 2 metres in height. It is possible that these two stones are contemporary with the circle, but they could just as easily have been later additions. The stones are aligned north-east to south-west and thus could have been erected to mark either the midsummer sunrise or midwinter sunset, or perhaps both these astronomical events. It is also interesting to note that the northern stone of this pair, which is known as the 'Dreaming Stone', possesses magnetic qualities and curiously, as Philip Burton has remarked, if a person of average height was to sit on the ledge that can be seen on the bottom of the stone, the magnetic areas would be immediately behind them on either side of their head. The summit of Carn Ingli, which lies some 6.5 miles to the north-west of Gors Fawr also contains areas of magnetic rock; in some cases the magnetism is so strong that it can make a compass needle spin round 360°. Several magnetic megaliths are known in other parts of Wales; for example, in my own area of special interest – the Llŷn peninsula – the Betws Fawr standing stone and one of the supporting stones of the Myndd Cefnamwlch Neolithic tomb are magnetic. Were these megaliths deliberately chosen because the prehistoric people who erected them could somehow detect their magnetic properties and thus saw them as being 'magical' in some way? Or, as seems more likely, can we simply put down their inclusion in monuments to coincidence?

Interestingly, the Reverend W. D. Bushell, writing in the Welsh archaeological journal, *Archaeologia Cambrensis* (1911), mentions the existence of an avenue at Gors Fawr, leading from the circle to the above two standing stones. Thus, this pair of stones may well have acted as a gateway or 'portal' into the circle, with people passing through it and processing down the avenue to the circle to perform rituals and ceremonies within its stones. Unfortunately, however, this avenue seems to have long since disappeared.

The location of Gors Fawr means that there are superb views to be had of the Preseli Hills, which ring the circle in a natural arc. In particular, the Carn Meini ridge can be seen rising above the centre of the circle to the north-east and its sharp and craggy outcrops were etched sharply against the clear blue sky the first time I visited the site. This probable referencing of Carn Meini (and the possible inclusion of stones from its summit in the circle) by the builders of Gors Fawr is likely to have been a deliberate act on their part, as it is evident that this was a very special place for the people who lived here during the prehistoric period. Perhaps the greatest support for this idea is provided by the eighty or so 'bluestones' (so-called because of the distinctive colour of the rock) that were set up inside Stonehenge and which, for the most part, were probably quarried from the rock outcrop of Carn Menyn on the summit of Carn Meini. Although not all agree that the bluestones were transported by people, and instead favour the idea of glacial action to explain their presence at Stonehenge, the general archaeological view is that the bluestones were indeed transported a staggering 155 miles to Salisbury Plain in an amazing act of prehistoric ingenuity and endurance. However, while many archaeologists are in agreement as to the source of the bluestones (or 'sources' – it is perhaps possible that some of the bluestones were brought from other parts of Wales such as the Brecon Beacons, (*Brycheiniog*), Snowdonia (*Eryri*) and even the Llŷn peninsula) the widely accepted date of their arrival and erection at Stonehenge (*c.*2550–2200 BC) has recently been questioned by two leading British archaeologists, Mike Pitts and Mike Parker Pearson of the Stonehenge Riverside Project. There are fifty-six 'Aubrey Holes' at Stonehenge, which are thought to be the post-holes of a timber circle that was located inside the earthwork enclosure (or henge), which date to the earliest pre-stone phase of Stonehenge (*c.*3000 BC). Instead, Pitts and Parker Pearson feel that judging from appearances the 'postholes' are more likely to have held a bluestone circle that is contemporary with the henge, and that along with stones from another possible bluestone circle recently found near Stonehenge on the banks of the River Avon, they were later used in the bluestone settings that date to the mid-third millennium BC (the time when Stonehenge was being transformed into the awesome stone circle that is so familiar to us today).

In addition to the location of Gors Fawr and the removal of the bluestones from Carn Menyn, recent fieldwork by the SPACES (Strumble-Preseli Ancient Communities and Environment Study) team led by professors Timothy Darvill and Geoffrey Wainwright has identified that numerous other Late prehistoric monuments such as Neolithic tombs, single standing stones and rock art panels cluster around Carn Meini in the wider landscape. Such archaeological evidence provides further credibility to the idea that this part of the landscape was of considerable significance to its prehistoric communities; it seems likely that this was because it was deemed to be a highly sacred area that was greatly revered. In fact, the Reverend Bushell was probably not that far from the truth when he wrote: 'Prescelly is unique. It seems, indeed, to have been a sort of prehistoric Westminster'.

It is clear that the true ideology that lay behind this reverence will always escape us, but could it be possible that Carn Meini was associated with some type of awesome mythological being by the prehistoric communities who lived in this area (and perhaps by those who lived further afield)? With this admittedly very speculative idea in mind, it is interesting that from a distance the Carn Meini ridge does bear some resemblance to the spine of some mighty dragon. In this regard, it is perhaps worth noting part of the creation myth of the American Lakota Indians, which refers to a similar landscape as Carn Menyn: 'Unktehi, the big water monster, was also turned to stone ... Her bones are in the Badlands now. Her back forms a long high ridge, and you can see her vertebrae sticking out in a great row of red and yellow rocks. I have seen them'. However, as interesting as such insights are in regard to the 'primitive' perception of the landscape, it is probably more likely that the Carn Meini ridge and in particular, the main outcrop of Carn Menyn

Llandudno Eisteddfod Gorsedd Circle
(Graham Tickner)

Porthmadog Eisteddfod Gorsedd Circle
(Graham Tickner)

Eglwys Gwyddelod, near Tywyn above the Dyfi estuary

Gors Fawr, near Mynachlog-ddu, Pembrokeshire

34

Pair of Standing Stones near Gors Fawr

The 'Dreaming Stone'

Bedd Arthur
(Dr Peter Hodges)

Carn Menyn

Dyffryn Syfynwy
(Graham Tickner)

Meini Gŵyr
(Graham Tickner)

*Bluestone pillar brought down from Carn Menyn
by RAF Chinook helicopter*

Churchyard gate, Ysbyty Cynfyn

Standing Stone in churchyard wall, Ysbyty Cynfyn

Largest Standing Stone in churchyard wall, Ysbyty Cynfyn
(Graham Tickner)

Cerrig Gaerau

Large stones at Ceri Hill

Smaller stones at Ceri Hill

Central recumbent stone at Ceri Hill

41

Larger Circle, Trecastle Mountain

Nant Tarw
© RCAHMW

Cerrig Duon, in the Brecon Beacons not far from Llandeilo

The Four Stones, Walton Basin near New Radnor

Early Bronze Age barrow near the Four Stones

Saith Maen Stone Row in the Brecon Beacons
(Dr Peter Hodges)

View south-east from Cerrig Arthur, above Barmouth

Maen Mawr and two-stone 'row'

Llyn Eiddew Bach, near Bryn Cader Faner, Ardudwy

Possible grave at Llyn Eiddew Bach

Moel Goedog West, above Harlech, Ardudwy

Moel Goedog East

Bedd Gorfal, above Harlech

Standing Stone
near Ardudwy Trackway

47

Dyffryn Ardudwy burial chambers

Bryn Cader Faner, Ardudwy

was worshipped because it was believed to be the home of supernatural forces.

It would not be particularly surprising if the Carn Meini ridge was probably viewed in this way by prehistoric people, as even from a modern viewpoint it has a fantastical quality that is hard to ignore. A visit to this place remains long in the memory. Christopher Catling has likened it, when seen from afar, to the walls and towers of some ancient ruined city. His description of a visit to the actual summit captures the powerful and mysterious quality of this unique place:

> (Carn Meini) has the atmosphere of a liminal place between earth and sky [which] is enhanced by the evocative primordial shapes of the rocky outcrops that form the 'walls' and 'towers' of this city in the clouds. In particular, the portal-like stone pillars at the top of... Carn Menyn, evoke the Lion Gate at Mycenae, though here they are entirely the result of the sculptural forces of frost, wind and rain. In between the tumbled rocks are fern-fringed water channels, deep crevices and shadowy holes suggestive of caves, tunnel entrances and openings into the underworld.

In addition to the striking nature of the rock formations found on the Carn Meini ridge, the actual rock itself contains some unusual qualities which might have had a 'magical' significance to the prehistoric people who encountered it. As well as being a striking greenish blue colour (hence the name 'bluestone') when freshly quarried and wet, this type of rock (dolerite) contains striking spots and flecks of white feldspar, which may have been seen as the stars on earth, or linked to some myth, as suggested by Tim Darvill. Furthermore, it is apparent that bluestone has an unusual sonic quality as when struck with a hammerstone it produces a ring like a bell or gong, and can even sound like a drum.

Thus bluestones that may have been seen as being 'supernaturally-charged' could have been quarried from Carn Menyn and then transported a huge distance to Salisbury Plain, where they transformed the early phase of Stonehenge. Tim Darvill has also come up with an intriguing theory in regard to exactly why the bluestones were included in an important religious monument that lay many miles away on Salisbury Plain. He has suggested that they were transported to Stonehenge because it was believed that the bluestones possessed the power to heal the sick and the diseased. Interestingly, Geoffrey of Monmouth's twelfth-century *Historia Regum Britanniae* ('History of Britain') tells of how Merlin brought the stones to Stonehenge by transporting a stone circle from Ireland (Geoffrey identified Ireland as the source of the stones on the basis of earlier writings, which mentioned that the stones had been brought to Stonehenge from a land far to the west) and that these stones were believed to have healing powers. While such ancient writings should obviously be treated with caution, they may nevertheless contain garbled traces of the truth handed down from generation to generation in an oral tradition that could be thousands of years old. It may be interesting to note that in the Preseli Hills region there is still a folk belief that the bluestones have healing qualities and many of the springs and wells of this area are viewed in a similar fashion. In addition to this belief, possible prehistoric 'holy wells' have also been identified by Darvill and Wainwright around Carn Menyn, where natural springs have apparently been modified by enlarging them and by enclosing them with low walls.

Bedd Arthur ('Arthur's grave')

This somewhat unique monument is located about 2 miles north of Gors Fawr and sits next to an important prehistoric trackway that runs along the top of the Preseli Hills from Cwm Gwaun to Crymych. The site lies close to Carn Menyn, and seen from here, the rock outcrops on Carn Meini's summit look as though they have just erupted out of the earth, their dark colouring contrasting strongly with the green of the grass-covered slopes. Although Bedd Arthur is not strictly a true circle and is in fact more oval, or boat-shaped, it is nevertheless of some importance as it provides some support for the idea that prehistoric people from the Preseli Hills were responsible for, or at the least were involved in, the transformation of Stonehenge into the awesome monument that still stands today, some five thousand years after its construction.

Bedd Arthur consists of seventeen bluestone pillars that are arranged in an oval that measures some 20 metres by 9 metres and which has its long axis aligned in a north–easterly-south-westerly direction (this alignment may well be of possible astronomical significance). It is also apparent that its builders

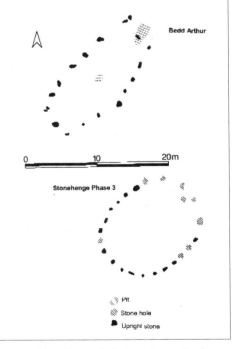

Bedd Arthur and the Stonehenge Oval (redrawn after Darvill and Wainwright)

cut a level platform into the slope on which the stones stand and these seem to be graded in height, with the tallest at the south-western end. A depression at the north-eastern end probably marks the position of a former standing stone, as may another depression in the middle of the monument.

The most fascinating aspect of Bedd Arthur is that it bears a close resemblance to the inner bluestone 'horseshoe' at Stonehenge that was erected in the last half of the third millennium BC. Although the Stonehenge horseshoe is wider than Bedd Arthur and features more stones, it has the same axial alignment as the latter, its twenty-four bluestones were graded in height from the north-east to south-west, and a standing stone was also probably once located at its north-eastern end. As Tim Darvill has plausibly argued in regard to the striking similarities that can be seen between these monuments: 'The two must be closely connected, if not the work of the same people'.

In further respect of the idea that people from the Preseli Hills were closely involved in the transportation and erection of the bluestones at Stonehenge, we must also briefly consider here a remarkable discovery that was made near Stonehenge in 2003. At Boscombe Down airfield, archaeologists discovered a normal-sized grave in which seven people had been buried: three adult males, a teenage male and three children, one of whom had been cremated. Analysis of the men's skulls and that of the teenager strongly indicated that they were related. Five barbed and tanged arrowheads (which led to occupants of the grave being named the 'Boscombe Bowmen'), some flint tools, a boar's tusk and a collection of eight Beaker pots were found accompanying the dead and these artefacts dated the burial to the period *c.*2600–2000 BC. To find so many people in a grave of this time is highly unusual (individual burial was the norm during this period), as were the Beakers themselves, which were of the early type known as 'AOC' or 'All Over Cord'. These Beakers are rare in Britain and more commonly found in Europe and one Beaker in particular showed strong affinities with European examples. In addition to this ceramic evidence for continental connections, a bone toggle that would have been worn on clothing in some fashion (perhaps used for fastening a cloak) was also found in the grave. These items are even rarer in Britain than AOC Beakers and again, are commonly found in European Beaker graves.

Therefore, the evidence found with the Boscombe Bowmen shows firm links with continental Europe and thus it is quite possible that they were immigrants who arrived in Britain at some point in the mid-third millennium BC. However, strontium isotope analysis on the Bowmen's tooth enamel provided intriguing results which could

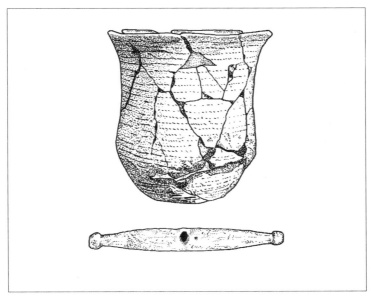

AOC Beaker and bone toggle found with 'Boscombe Bowmen'

indicate otherwise. (Strontium isotopes are locked into tooth enamel through drinking water and provide a chemical 'fingerprint' for the areas in which people lived.) The analysis showed that the Bowmen's teeth contained very high levels of strontium and that these strontium levels could be closely matched in rocks found in Scotland, the Lake District and, intriguingly, Wales. Thus, as Wales lies closest to the grave of the Bowmen and Stonehenge, the idea that these were members of a 'Welsh' community who were actually involved in the transportation of the Bluestones from the Preseli Hills is one that becomes attractive. However, Alison Sheridan has recently argued that it is more probable that the Boscombe Bowmen actually came from Brittany. It is also not beyond the bounds of possibility that their homeland lay in south-east Ireland, the Massif Central of France, the Black Forest region of Germany, or even Portugal. We will never know what the truth is behind the compelling glimpse of prehistoric migration that the Boscombe Bowmen have left us, but the possibility remains that the driving force behind the construction of one of the world's greatest prehistoric monuments was a group who hailed from the Preseli Hills.

The Eithbedd ('gorse-grave') circles

These three circles, which are unfortunately now destroyed, were surveyed and reported in *Archaeologia Cambrensis* (1911) by the Reverend W. D. Bushell, a man of the church who it seems, also had archaeological leanings. It is evident that he was very keen in examining possible astronomical alignments (particularly stellar ones) at the stone circles he visited in the Preseli Hills, as shown by the following somewhat impenetrable passage (at least to those of us who are not astronomers) relating to the Dyffryn Syfynwy circle:

From E, allowing for a slight elevation of the sky-line, we infer a southern declination of about 11° 30', a declination which would of itself suggest a Aquarii, a Ceti, and a Scorpionis (*Antares*) in B.C. 1100, B.C. 1150, and B.C. 1650 respectively. I do not find however that the first two of these would be of any use as warning stars [to herald the approach of dawn].

Mr Bushell tells us that the Eithbedd circles were located about 1.5 miles to the south-west of 'Prescelly Top' in the parish of Maenclochog and although it is not exactly clear where the circles were located it seems likely that they were close to the field marked as 'Eithbed', which lies just to the north of Maenclochog (083273/145). If we are to believe his account of the circles (which even in his day were in sorry condition and thus he may have misinterpreted these sites), Circle C was very large, with a diameter of no less than around 45 metres, while Circle B was about half the size of the former monument and may have had a burial chamber standing at its centre. As to Circle A, Mr Bushell tells us that it was 'carried off in 1905 to build a wall'. Near to the edge of Circle B, there was a curious low, narrow mound that was dug into by Warin Foster Bushell (Mr Bushell's son). The results of this 'excavation' were disappointing however, as all he found was a rough pavement of stones and a small quantity of black ashes, which may represent a ceremonial fire that was lit prior to the building of the barrow.

Dyffryn Syfynwy
This circle is set in a picturesque location high on the western bank of the Afon Syfynwy some 5 miles south-west of Bedd Arthur. The circle is slightly oval in shape, measuring 22 by 19 metres in diameter with its long axis

orientated south-west to north-east. When Mr Bushell visited the site as part of his tour of the Preseli circles, some ten or eleven stones out of an original eighteen were still in their original positions. Today, many of the stones (around 1–2 m in height) are toppled and the site is rather ruinous, but it is still clear that when it was in use this circle would have been a fairly imposing monument. The faint remains of a burial cairn can still be made out within the centre of the circle, but its contents have long since gone, no doubt plundered by those who were seeking 'treasure' rather than knowledge.

Meini Gwŷr ('soldiers' stones') or Buarth Arthur ('Arthur's enclosure')

When complete, this would have been an impressive example of what is known as an 'embanked' stone circle. It is just one of several monuments that form an important prehistoric ritual and ceremonial complex close to the hamlet of Glandy Cross, which lies about 2 miles south of Gors Fawr. Unfortunately, only two stones of the circle now remain but there were probably originally seventeen, although it should be noted that the famous eighteenth-century Welsh antiquarian, Edward Lhuyd, claimed that there were twenty-three. The low enclosing bank of turf, clay and stones is now denuded, but it can still clearly be seen, standing around 1 metre high in some places. The stone circle was about 18 metres in diameter, while the bank enclosing it measured some 37 metres. An entrance measuring around 3 metres wide can also still be observed in the north-west section of the bank. An excavation was carried out at the site by W. F. Grimes in the summer of 1938 and although the finds from this investigation were rather meagre, he did find pottery sherds from Early Bronze Age Food Vessels and evidence of a fire-pit in front of the entrance.

Other sites of interest

Even a brief look at this area on the map shows how rich
north Pembrokeshire is in prehistoric remains. A fascinating
and diverse collection of prehistoric monuments can be
found among its beautiful landscapes. Of particular note are
the spectacular Iron Age hillfort on Foel Drygarn
(158336/145 – this site also has three impressive Bronze
Age burial cairns located inside its ramparts) and the well-
known and superb Neolithic burial chamber of Pentre-Ifan
that lies about 5 miles to the north-west of Bedd Arthur. It is
also worth noting the fine bluestone pillar that was brought
down from the summit of Carn Menyn by an RAF Chinook
helicopter and set up near the carpark at the foot of Carn
Sian and many other standing stones can be found dotted
around this area.

Chapter 3

Stone circles of central/southern Wales

Ysbyty Cynfyn ('Cynfyn's hospice')

The small church known as Ysbyty Cynfyn and the possible prehistoric stone circle associated with it lies about 1.5 miles to the north-east of Devil's Bridge (*Pontarfynach*), which is renowned for its spectacular waterfalls that thousands of sightseers come to marvel at every year. The best (but not the quickest) way to reach this site is to take the former lead-miners' train that runs from Aberystwyth up the southern side of Cwm Rheidol, its steep, thickly wooded slopes and lush farmland creating what has to be one of the most pleasant and picturesque areas of Wales. Who Cynyfyn was remains unknown, but it is probable that he was a Cistercian monk or lay-brother who founded a hospice or rest-house on the site around 1200 AD, for medieval pilgrims who were travelling to the famous abbey of Strata Florida (*Ystrad Fflur*), about 16 miles away on the banks of the Teifi.

The wall of the churchyard stands on a roughly circular earthwork that surrounds the church and set into the wall are five standing stones. Two slender stones act as gateposts at the church entrance to the east, while just to the right of the gate two broad and squat standing stones are set into the wall, one of them partly hidden under a covering of moss when I visited the site. Behind these stones, to the north, is a truly magnificent standing stone that measures about 3.5 metres high, over 1 metre wide, and 0.5 metres thick. Many stone circle enthusiasts therefore believe that what we see today at Ysbyty Cynfyn represents the remains of an embanked stone circle that was incorporated into the later church in a typical example of the Christianisation of a former pagan site.

However, not all have subscribed to this view and in an article in *Archaeologia Cambrensis* (1979), C. S. Briggs raised a number of objections to the prehistoric authenticity of the circle. Firstly, he notes that the masonry of the wall passes below the gatepost stones and the other two nearby, and that there is no real evidence that these stones ever stood in the ground. Thus Briggs argues that this suggests that these four stones were brought from elsewhere when the current wall was built around the church, probably in the early nineteenth century. Next, he turns his attention to the discrepancies that crop up in the accounts of the site that appear in Benjamin Heath Malkin's 1804 and 1807 versions of *The Scenery, Antiquities and Biography of South Wales*. In the 1804 edition we are told that at Ysbyty Cynfyn 'There is in the churchyard a large, upright stone monument...I could not learn that any tradition was attached to it in the neighbourhood'. In the later edition Malkin writes: 'There are in the churchyard large upright stone monuments... The church has been built within a large druidical circle or temple'. As Briggs rightly points out, these discrepancies are odd, as is the fact that church records make no mention of a 'druidical' circle around the church and furthermore, eighteenth- and nineteenth-century maps showing Ysbyty Cynfyn do not provide any evidence of such a monument. He has also cast doubt on the huge monolith that stands in the northern wall and remarks that it is strange that it was not mentioned by eighteenth-century antiquarians who had passed by the church, when they had drawn attention to the equally impressive stone in the graveyard at Rudston church in the East Riding of Yorkshire.

It is quite possible then, that rather than representing

the remains of a stone circle, the standing stones at Ysbyty Cynfyn were added to the churchyard wall to prettify it, or to attract gullible tourists to the site, as Briggs suggests. Admittedly, the evidence does weigh in favour of this idea, but it does not prove that it is correct. At the least, it seems unlikely that the huge stone was a 'modern' addition to the site, as it is known to be in its original position and it certainly looks prehistoric. In fact, this standing stone may actually have been an outlier to a nearby stone circle and the possibility remains that the other standing stones in the wall represent the remnants of this. Of course, all the arguments for and against a prehistoric stone circle at Ysbyty Cynfyn are a matter of conjecture and the unfortunate truth is that we will probably never get to the bottom of the mystery surrounding the stones in the churchyard wall. Perhaps though, this does not matter, as this little church tucked away in a peaceful and secluded corner of central Wales is worth visiting purely for its idyllic beauty.

Eglyws Gwyddelod ('church of the Irishman')
This small, but fine monument is located at the junction of two prehistoric trackways in the hills that rise above the lovely Dyfi estuary. During the summer months, when lush grass and ferns have grown around the stones, it is quite hard to spot them and unless you were looking for the circle, you could easily walk past and miss it. The circle sits on an elevated spur of land and commands splendid views of the dark, tree-covered hills and farmland that lie to the north-east of the Dyfi valley. Today, Eglyws Gwddelod consists of seven stones (two of these are low stumps), although there may have been eight stones originally. There may also have been a burial cairn in the centre of the circle, though this is far from certain and if there was, it could have been a later addition to the site. The name of this monument also tempts

one to speculate whether it preserves a folk memory of who was actually buried here, with a renowned Bronze Age traveller from across the Irish Sea perhaps being laid to rest in this lonely but beguiling spot. A number of other prehistoric monuments in Wales are attributed to 'Gwddelod' or 'Irishmen' and although of course, this could simply be a convenient label given to sites of unknown origin it is worth bearing in mind the proximity of Wales to Ireland. There was undoubtedly contact between Irish and Welsh communities in

Plan of Eglwys Gwyddelod
(redrawn after Hoyle)

prehistoric times and it would hardly be surprising if, sometimes, members of Irish communities crossed the Irish Sea and settled in Wales (and vice-versa).

Cerrig Gaerau ('stones of the hillforts') and Lled-Croen-yr-Ych ('the width of the ox-hide')

These two curious circles are located in a remote location on the flat summit of Newydd Fynddog which, although somewhat bleak in aspect, nevertheless provides the visitor with magnificent views of the distinctive and captivating central Welsh countryside. The two monuments stand about 130 metres apart with Cerrig Gaerau at the south-west and Lled-Croen-yr-Ych to the north-east. The former circle consists of eight larger than average stones which although now prostrate, may have once stood upright in a circle measuring 21 metres in diameter. It would not be unfair to describe Lled-Croen-Yr-Ych as unimpressive, as it now consists of five low, boulders partly hidden by marshy grass, which form an oval measuring about 25 x 23 metres.

A number of hollows can be observed in the circle's circumference and these could mark the position of former stones that were removed at some point in the past. About 30 metres to the south-east there is a low outlying stone that once stood upright. It is conceivable that this stone was set up so that it was in line with the rising midsummer sun. As we will see in the following pages, several other Welsh stone circles feature outlying standing stones and it is quite probable that many of these stones were likewise erected as markers of astronomical events. As to the strange name given to the circle, Aubrey Burl has noted that it 'derives from a belief that this was the burial place of a bereaved-ox' whose hide was stretched out and enclosed in the stone circle (although of what or whom it was bereaved is unclear!). How far back this curious belief reaches is unclear, but it is quite possible that it is prehistoric in origin. Similar stories are associated with the Maiden Bower Neolithic causewayed enclosure and Iron Age hillfort in Bedfordshire.

The reason why the circles differ markedly in appearance remains hidden with their long-dead builders, but it is

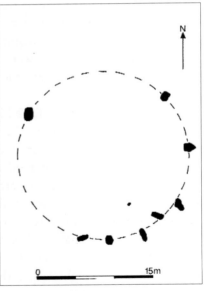

Plan of Cerrig Gaerau
(redrawn after Hoyle)

perhaps possible that they were used for different rituals that required their own separate space. However, it may be more probable that one circle succeeded another and that different communities were responsible for their construction. An intriguing thought in this regard, is the possibility that the flat stones of Cerrig Gaerau were actually toppled over in a hostile act by the builders of Lled-Croen-Yr-Ych. Such ideas are, of

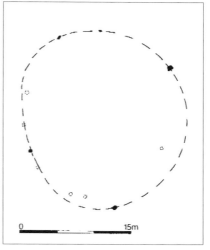

Plan of Lled-Croen-yr-Ych (redrawn after Hoyle)

course, speculative, but there is plentiful evidence from the archaeological record which shows that life in prehistoric Britain was far removed from the golden idyll still envisaged by some and that violence and warfare were no strangers to the people who made up its communities.

Ceri Hill

This unusual circle is located on Ceri Hill near Newtown (*Drenewydd*) and is situated just to the south of the Ceri Ridgeway – another important route dating back to prehistoric times that linked the Irish Sea with the Severn Basin at least as far back as the Early Bronze Age. It is a large monument (about 26 m in diameter) and consists of nine low-lying stones, and among these are two rather curious stones – one pointed and one flat-topped – in the eastern arc of the circle. It is possible, perhaps, that these two stones are female and male symbols, as has been suggested for

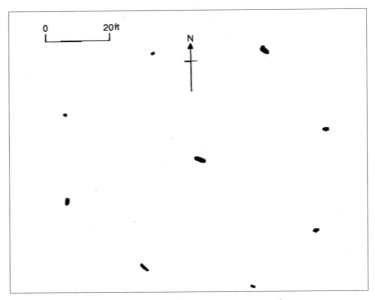

Plan of Ceri Hill (redrawn after Thom)

other pairs of standing stones of contrasting shape that are common in Wales, Scotland and Ireland (though often these are much larger in size). In the centre of the circle is a broad, recumbent stone around 1 metre in height and this may cover a cremation burial, as is commonly found at circles with centre stones in south-west Scotland and south-west Ireland. There has been some suggestion that the Ceri Hill circle is a modern fake, though its location near a prehistoric trackway and the existence of Bronze Age burial mounds nearby, suggest that the circle formed part of a prehistoric ritual and ceremonial landscape. We would also have to question why someone in more recent times would want to go the great trouble of erecting a stone circle in this rather remote location.

Carneddau Hengwm, Neolithic tomb in Ardudwy

Druids' Circle, above Penmaenmawr

Druids' Circle

Circle 278 on Cefn Coch moorland above Penmaenmawr

Monument 280 with Graig Lwyd in background

Ring cairn near Druids' Circle

Circle 275 on Cefn Coch moorland above Penmaenmawr

Red Farm on Cefn Coch moorland above Penmaenmawr

'Playing Card' Standing Stone near Red Farm

Maen-y-Bardd burial chamber, Dyffryn Conwy

Cerrig Pryfaid, on the Roman Road near Llanfairfechan

Tyfos Uchaf, in the hills above Llandrillo

Tyfos Uchaf, looking towards Moel-Tŷ-Uchaf

Moel-Tŷ-Uchaf, above Llandrillo

Cist grave at Moel-Tŷ-Uchaf

Brenig 44

Brenig 51

Brenig 8

Brenig 51, central circle

Brenig 51, semi-circle cairn

Penbedw Parc, near Mold

*Standing Stone
near Penbedw Parc circle*

Entrance at Bryn Celli Ddu

Bryn Celli Ddu, Môn
(Graham Tickner)

Y Capel

This is another circle near Newtown, but frustratingly, I was not able to locate it during my research for this book. This is unsurprising as Frances and Jacob Butler, who were the first people to survey and record the site in 1978, tell us that the fifty-four small stones of the circle, which is around 25 metres in diameter, are located among long tussocks of coarse moorland grass. Thus, this circle would only really be easy to spot from a close distance and as at Eglwys Gwydellod, one could easily walk past the site without noticing it (a problem not uncommon at several other Welsh stone circles!).

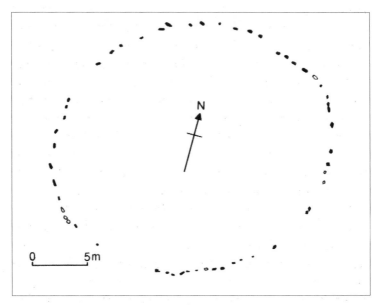

Plan of Y Capel
(redrawn after Butler and Butler)

Trecastle Mountain

These two circles are located in a wild and lonely area of high moorland that lies about 4 miles to the south-east of the pleasant town of Llandovery (*Llanymddyfri*) (once an important centre for drovers moving cattle between Wales and England and also the site of a ruined medieval castle built by the Normans in the twelfth-century) which is located on the north-eastern edge of the Brecon Beacons National Park (*Parc Cenedlaethol Brycheiniog*). Fine views of the rolling hills and farmland of the Brecon Beacons unfurl before you as you climb up on to Trecastle Mountain. On my first visit to the circles just after sunrise on an August morning, I was rewarded with a view of serene beauty that remains etched in my memory. The circles stand close to the remains of two Roman marching camps (faint traces of their earthworks can still be made out) and the former Roman road that runs across the moor. They stand south-west and north-east of each other, and show a considerable contrast in size, with their diameters measuring about 7.5 and 23 metres respectively. Alexander Thom felt that the larger of the circles was aligned on the midwinter sunrise. An unimpressive, but enigmatic row of four low boulders (about 18 m long) runs towards the smaller circle from the south-west and a fallen standing stone can be seen nearby to the south-east. Writing in the early nineteenth century, Lt-Col. W. Llewellyn–Morgan proposed that this row was aligned towards sunset in early February and November (the time of the Celtic festivals of Imbolc and Samhain). A denuded mound within the larger circle probably marks the remains of a Bronze Age burial cairn. As at Cerrig Gaerau and Lled-Croen-Yr-Ych, one circle may have succeeded another, with different communities perhaps involved in their construction.

Cerrig Duon ('black rocks')

This captivating and rather special monument is situated in a dramatic and imposing landscape of great beauty and provides us with one of the clearest examples of how stone circle builders often deliberately positioned their monuments in natural arenas formed by hills and mountains. Cerrig Duon is positioned on a flat-topped spur of land that rises above the Tawe and this spur almost looks as though it was deliberately built to accommodate the circle. The lower reaches of the famous Mynydd Ddu ('black mountain') sweep down to enclose the circle in the narrow pass of Bwlch Cerrig Duon, which runs from Trecastle (*Trecastell*) to Aber-craf. Any ceremonies and rituals that were performed within the confines of this marvellous site are likely to have had a considerable effect on the people who witnessed them. The low stones of the circle actually form an ovoid that measures about 20.5 by 18 metres, and 9 metres to the north of the circle is the fine standing stone known as Maen Mawr ('the great stone') that weighs a staggering 9 tons and measures 2 metres in height. As Aubrey Burl has suggested, this giant of a stone may well have been set up as a 'guidestone' or directional marker for prehistoric travellers moving through the pass. However, Alexander Thom also

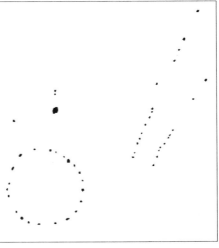

Plan of Cerrig Duon (redrawn after Burl)

made the suggestion that it indicated the rising position of the star Arcturus in 1950 BC. In line with Maen Mawr, about 0.5 metres to the north is a 'row' of two small stones that are dwarfed by their massive counterpart (32). The true function of these mysterious little stones remains forever hidden in the prehistoric past, but they may lend further support to Thom's theory, as it is clear that these stones would not have been visible form a distance. An intrig-uing double row of tiny stones also runs up to towards the circle from the river and although these are not particularly easy to discern amongst the thick vegetation it is evident that they mark an irregular avenue, with one row measuring nearly 25 metres in length and the other 45 metres. It is felt that this is a later addition to the monument, though its true purpose can only be guessed at. However, one such guess is that it was used as a ceremonial route that led from the sacred waters of the Tawe up to the circle (water from the river may well have been used in rituals and ceremonies carried out the circle). Dr Peter Hodges has also noted that to the north-west of the circle, there is a line of stones that appears to point in the direction of a four large and low stones. He has suggested, not unreasonably, that this combination of stones is a man-made arrangement that marks the midsummer sunset.

Nant Tarw ('the bull-brook')
A combination of bad map-reading, a lack of directions and failing light conspired against me to ensure that I was unable to visit this pair of circles located on a wide and flat expanse of bare and boggy moorland that lies between the above circle and those on Trecastle Mountain. The circles stand within 90 metres of each other in a natural ring of hills and the diameter of the north-western monument measures about 21 x 19 metres, while its south-eastern neighbour has

a diameter of around 21 x 18 metres. Alexander Thom proposed that the north-western ring may have been aligned on the setting of the star Spica in 1900 BC and that a central alignment through the two circles was orientated towards sunset on May Day and Lammas (corresponding with the Celtic festivals of Beltane and Lughnasa). Some 90 metres to the north-west of the circles is a setting of one large standing stone (now fallen) and two much smaller ones, which is reminiscent of the Maen Mawr group at Cerrig Duon. We could speculate that this indicates that the builders of the Nant Tarw were also responsible for the construction of Cerrig Duon, or more probably, that different prehistoric communities were exchanging religious ideas in this area of the Brecon Beacons.

Ynys-hir ('the long island')
I have not visited this circle, but those people who wish to do so should be aware that as it lies on the Sennybridge (*Pontsenni*) military training area, which is sometimes used as a firing range, it is imperative that written permission is sought first (stone circles are fascinating and rewarding places to visit but they are not worth dying for!). Ynys-Hir is located on Mynydd Epynt midway between Llandovery and Brecon (*Aberhonddu*). The monument lies at the intersection of two trackways that cross the mountain; with one linking the Usk valley near Sennybridge to the Cledan valley near Llanwrtyd Wells (*Llanwrtyd*), and the other a more local route that connects the Nant Brân valley to the Cileini valley. The circle's excavator, G. C. Dunning plausibly argued that these routeways are prehistoric in date and that the circle was deliberately positioned at their junction so any passing prehistoric travellers would be well aware of it.

It seems that even with Britain heavily involved in the

most destructive war of all time, archaeologists could still find time to pursue their passion, as the circle was excavated in June 1940. The stumps of five stones still in their original positions were uncovered, along with a further twelve that had fallen over. The stones had been arranged in a substantial circle of around 58 metres in diameter and as at Gors Fawr, they were graded in height with the stones increasing in size from north to south. A pit that may mark a grave was discovered near the centre of the circle, though no artefacts or skeletal material were found in it. The only finds to come from the circle were three flint flakes that had been used as prehistoric tools. It is perhaps also possible that a group of boulders incorporated in the south-east arc of the circle indicate the rising sun at midwinter.

As well as excavating Ynys-hir G. C. Dunning investigated a nearby burial cairn that turned out to be a rather interesting and complex monument. At the cairn's centre was a small and shallow burial pit covered by a slab of local sandstone, and at its base were fragments of cremated bone. Unfortunately, analysis of this bone was not able to determine the sex or age of the person it had come from. Surrounding this central burial was a wide and loosely-piled ring of boulders, which in

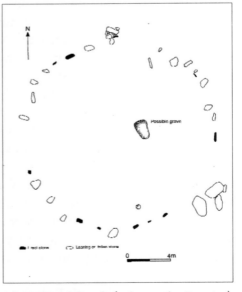

Plan of Ynys-hir circle (redrawn after Dunning)

turn was surrounded by a single ring of boulders that lay about 1 metre away. G. C. Dunning speculated that the outer circle of boulders had acted as a 'ritual boundary between those within, who assisted in making the burial at the centre of the circle and performed ceremonies around it, and those who remained outside this area, who were able to watch the rites but not allowed to take part in them'. Interestingly, the open space that lay between the outer and inner stone rings was found to be hard and compact, suggesting that people had processed or danced around this 'ritual pathway' (as Dunning called it).

Another cremation burial in a shallow, sandstone covered pit was discovered about 3 metres to the north-east of the central burial and the skull fragments appear to have

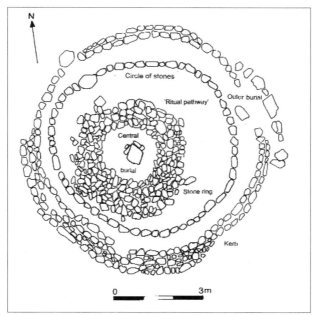

Plan of Ynys-hir cairn (redrawn after Dunning)

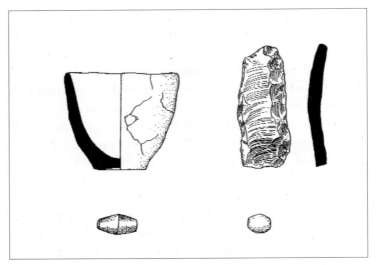

Grave goods from Ynys-hir cairn (redrawn after Dunning)

belonged to a youth, though again, their age or sex could not be determined. Interred with this individual were a Bronze Age 'Pygmy Cup' a flint knife and two beads. However, perhaps the most interesting of the finds were the four small fragments of woven material (probably wool) that probably belonged to some type of garment. This was an important and remarkable survival as, unsurprisingly, such finds are extremely rare in the British Isles.

The Four Stones

The Four Stones lie in an enchanting area of countryside (the Walton Basin) some 2 miles east of the village of New Radnor (*Maesyfed*), which lies close to the Shropshire border. These four impressive monoliths have been wrongly interpreted as the remains of a Neolithic burial chamber, or the remains of a partly ruined circle, when in fact they actually represent a Welsh example of 'Four-Poster' ring. This is a type of prehistoric monument that appears to have originated in Scotland (probably in Aberdeenshire), where there are two dense northern and southern concentrations of Four-Posters.

The stones are not particularly tall (around 1–1.5 m in height) but they are truly megalithic, with the heaviest stone weighing in at around 6 tons. This hefty monolith would have required around thirty people to lift it and therefore, this means that the erection of Maen Mawr at Cerrig Duon would have required well over this number. If the Four Stones did indeed come from Hanter Hill, as believed, they would certainly have provided a serious challenge to the people who brought them from here, as the hill lies around 2 miles from the site.

Strange prehistoric carvings known as 'cupmarks' (small circular depressions) are said to feature on the south-west stone, but unfortunately I forgot to look for these during a visit to the site on a memorable summer's day! It is interesting to note that the midwinter sun sets in the south-west, and also that at Llannerch farm some 5 miles from the Four Stones there is a boulder that bears thirty-two cupmarks. The tallest stone at the north-east may have been an indicator of sunrise on May Day and Lammas.

How a Scottish-style prehistoric monument came to be erected in mid-Wales remains a prehistoric mystery, but it is quite possible, as Aubrey Burl has suggested, that the isolated examples of four-posters found outside Scotland could represent the movement of emigrants searching for fertile agricultural land or copper ore for their tools and weapons. Alternatively, they may have been driven south by darker forces such as warfare or disease.

Local folklore has it that the stones mark the graves of four kings who lost their lives in a battle fought close by, and when these long-dead warriors hear the church bells they go to the nearby Hindwell pool to drink.

In addition to the Four Stones, the survival of several Bronze Age burial mounds and standing stones nearby, indicate that this area of the Walton Basin was revered by the prehistoric communities who left them in the landscape as memorials to their lives.

Llorfa

Llorfa stone circle lies some 10 miles south-west of Cerrig Duon and was discovered in June 2006 during fieldwork carried out by Clwyd-Powys Archaeological Trust. As with many Welsh circles, the stones of this monument actually form an ellipse (10.25 x 9.5 m) with its longest axis orientated east–west. The monument is located on a moorland ridge that runs between two remote upland valleys above the town of Ystradgynlais, on the southern edge of the Brecon Beacons. Characteristically, the circle

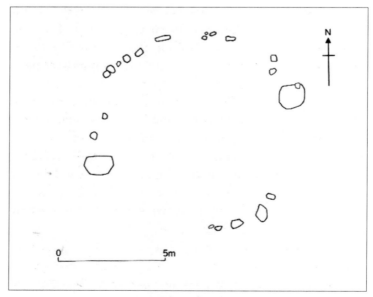

Plan of Llorfa (redrawn after Jones)

commands wide-ranging views and is enclosed by a natural arena of distant hills. The remaining twenty stones of the circle are small, with none reaching over 1 metre in height. Although it is hard to say for sure how many stones there originally were, it is very likely that several others lie hidden below the moorland peat and turf.

Crugiau Bach

Although as with the above site, this circle must have been known to local farmers and hardy walkers who had passed by it, Crugiau Bach was not recorded until 1979 by Clywd-Powys Archaeological Trust. It is located to the north-west of Llandrindod Wells on an area of remote moorland to the south-east of the Claerwen valley, near the village of Llanwrthwl. Today, the circle (around 24 m in diameter) is comprised of twenty-one stones, although investigations at the site suggested that the circle probably originally comprised at least fifty stones and that many now lie hidden below the blanket of peat that covers the moorland. A low-standing stone can be found about 75 metres to the north-east of the circle and between 60–120 metres to the west of the circle; the remains of several small cairns and the remains of an oval enclosure are also visible. It is quite possible that the cairns cover burials and that the enclosure was ceremonial in nature. Therefore, together with the stone circle, they may have formed part of a prehistoric religious complex. However, it is also possible that the cairns and the enclosure are related to agricultural, rather than religious, activity, though their proximity to the circle perhaps argues against this idea.

Other sites of interest

About 3 miles north of Ysbyty Cynfyn is the Hirnant cairn circle (753839/135) and several Bronze Age burial mounds and cairns are located near to Eglwys Gwdddelod, Cerrig Gaerau, Lled-Croen-yr-Ych, and Ceri Hill. About 3 miles south of Cerrig Duon are the stunning Dan-yr-Ogof show caves, which are well worth a visit. One of the caves (the 'Bone Cave') was used as a burial chamber by prehistoric communities in the area, with many skeletons dating to the Bronze Age found, along with scores of deer bones (dated to *c.*7000 BC) from the Mesolithic period. High above Dan-yr-Ogof, there is the fascinating Saith Maen ('seven stones') prehistoric stone row (834154/160). Other examples of stone rows can be found in Wales and although their purpose is unknown, it is quite possible that they were set up as markers of astronomical events.

Chapter 4

Stone circles of north-western Wales

Cerrig Arthur ('Arthur's stones')
This monument is located about 2 miles north-east of the popular holiday resort of Barmouth (*Abermo*) on the western coast of the Snowdonia National Park (*Parc Cenedlaethol Eryri*). The circle lies above Barmouth and as you follow the narrow lane that takes you to it, you are presented with a glorious view of the Mawddach sinuously winding its way into the heart of Snowdonia, its broad, silvery loops and wide sand flats overlooked by the majestic Cadair Idris; this is surely one of the finest views in Britain, if not anywhere.

As at so many other Welsh circles, there is a feeling of being in a natural arena at this site, with the distant hills and mountains of Snowdonia encircling it. Once again, we are drawn to the idea that circles were deliberately positioned in the landscape so that they had wide ranging views of its sacred places. From the circle there are impressive views to the north-east, with upland sheep-farming country and the dark mass of Craig-y-Cledd forest seen below the site, while to the south-east Cadair Idris looms magnificently on the horizon. Today, it is quite hard to make sense of the circle, although originally, the remaining stones formed part of an oval that measured around 16 x 13 metres. The longest axis of this oval ran from south-west to north-east and John Hoyle feels that it was deliberately orientated on the distant escarpment of Craig-y-llyn on the south-western shoulder of Cadair Idris, where, in 1700 BC, the moon at its most

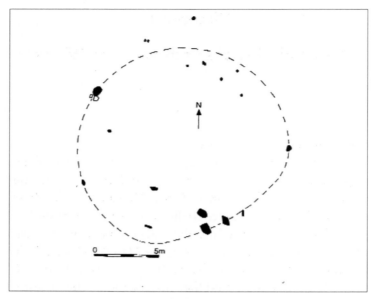

Plan of Cerrig Arthur (redrawn after Hoyle)

southerly position would have risen. It may also be interesting to note that a burial cairn can be seen on Craig-y-llyn and it is possible, perhaps, that there is some connection between the two monuments.

The builders of Cerrig Arthur created an artificial platform on which to locate the stones of the circle and these may have been surrounded by an earthen bank. The three large stones that form a group in the southern arc of the circle are intriguing as two of them appear to 'frame' the south-western summit of Cadair Idris, although it is hard to say for certain if they are in their original position. If they are, however, could it be possible that they also had some link with the moon as it raised its ghostly face above Cadair Idris some four thousand years ago?

Ffridd Newydd ('new pasture')

Today, little remains of these two circles and I would only really recommend that truly dedicated 'circle hunters' visit them. Nevertheless, we do know something of their original appearance, thanks to O. G. S Crawford (the famous pioneer of aerial photography in archaeology and one of the founders of modern, British archaeology) who surveyed and excavated them on behalf of the Cambrian Archaeological Association from early July to late September 1919. He tells us in the account of the work that appears in *Archaeologia Cambrensis* in 1920: 'I arrived at Hengwm [the old name for the site was Carneddau Hengwm – 'cairns in the old valley'] on July 2 and set up the tent in which I lived from July 7 to the end of September… The work was favoured by exceptionally fine weather'. For Crawford it must have been a rather lonely but idyllic existence, living in the uplands above Barmouth for seven weeks. We can imagine him sitting outside his tent in the cool of the evening, drinking a cup of tea (or something stronger, perhaps!) while enjoying the peace and solitude of the surrounding countryside, after a long and tiring day digging the circles with his team of local workmen in the late summer heat. Crawford also mentions that he and his workmen were plagued by flies during the excavations and having visited the uplands above Barmouth during the summer months on several occasions, this is a complaint that I can relate to!

The excavations revealed that two ditched and embanked circles had stood close to each other and that the largest circle (Circle T) was around 50 metres in diameter with 45–50 low stones that were set curiously on the outer edge of the bank. A strange V-shaped trench was also discovered running across the centre of the circle, though what its purpose was, and whether it was prehistoric or modern in date, could not be fathomed. Finds were scanty within the circle, although some rough pottery sherds of uncertain date were discovered underneath a fallen upright and a curious small stone box containing the remains of a fire were found just outside the circle. It is probable that this latter evidence related to ritual activity carried out at the site during the time when it was functioning as a prehistoric religious monument.

The other circle (Circle S) was smaller than its neighbour, with a diameter of around 35 m. No stone uprights were found during the excavation of this circle, though this can probably be put down to local farmers using the circle as a ready source of building material. As at Circle T, finds were few, but traces of a fire-pit, probably connected with the religious rites performed here, were discovered. Close to the fire-pit, thirteen pottery sherds from a Copper Age 'rusticated Beaker' were unearthed and an oblong pit found in the centre of the circle may have been a grave. However, the lack of skeletal material in it suggested otherwise, although it is quite possible that the extremely acidic soils of this area had long since dissolved any traces of the individual who may have been buried here.

Bryn Cader Faner ('outlook post on the hill')
This superb and unique circle is one Wales' most notable prehistoric monuments and indeed, one of the finest in Britain. It lies above Harlech in a stark but striking area of boggy pastures, dark rocky ridges and secretive mountain tarns. The monument is sited on a dominant spur of land that rises above the well-known Ardudwy trackway – unsurprisingly, another trackway that has roots stretching back into prehistory. From the site there are superb views of the peaks of north-western Snowdonia rising above the estuary of the Glaslyn. As the circle is approached along the trackway, it forms a striking silhouette on its low hill and

there can be little doubt that this was the desired intention of those who built this stunning and dramatic monument.

In its present state, Bryn Cader Faner consists of fifteen tall and pointed pillars all around 2 metres long (there may have been as many as thirty pillars originally), which lean outwards from the central cairn at a marked angle. At the centre of the cairn the remains of a damaged cist grave can be seen, its contents unfortunately long since pillaged by nineteenth-century robbers (who knows what they might have found in this special monument?).

The sequence of building events at Bryn Cader Faner is, it must be said, far from certain. However, it is perhaps more probable that the standing stones mark the first phase of the monument, with the cairn added later, the weight of its stones pushing the long, narrow pillars outwards. Sadly, the monument was badly damaged by soldiers during the Second World War, who broke and pulled out stones from the circle in a mindless act of vandalism.

Llyn Eiddew Bach ('the little ivy lake')

This mysterious little ring of stones can be seen just next to the track that leads to Bryn Cader Faner, which is located about half a mile away to the north-east. Today, the circle is incomplete and only seven low stones of an original thirteen or fourteen remain, looking small and insignificant in the marshy ground that runs below the dark, looming crags and ridges of Moel Ysgyfarnogod. In the centre of the circle, a small stone-lined depression can be seen and this looks suspiciously like a grave, although curiously, no mention of this is made in any of the literature on the site. The circle takes its name from the nearby mountain tarn that sits like a little jewel amongst this bare and inhospitable mountain country.

Moel Goedog ('Goedog hill') West

While this 'circle' can perhaps be more correctly classified as a 'Complex Ring Cairn', as its excavator, Frances Lynch has pointed out, its exact classification is difficult and it could also be seen as an example of an embanked circle. However, we should not be overly concerned with the true architectural nature of this monument, as it has yielded fascinating evidence of Bronze Age funerary practices.

Like Bryn Cader Faner, Moel Goedog West is located next to the Ardudwy trackway, which comes up from the coast near Llanbedr to cross the mountains into the Trawsfynydd basin, about 5 miles to the north-east. The builders of Moel Goedog West levelled the interior of the circle by cutting back into the hill on the south-east, and as Frances Lynch has suggested, this was probably done 'so as to provide an appropriate platform for ceremonies' that took place within the circle. We can now only imagine these ceremonies, but the Glasyn Estuary, the mountains of Snowdonia and the long, narrow arm of the distant Llŷn Peninsula jutting out into the Irish Sea would have provided a marvellous backdrop.

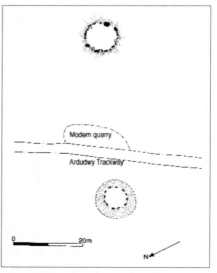

Plan of Moel Goedog cairn circle (redrawn after Lynch)

The monument itself consists of a ring of twelve low uprights (none over 1m high) that are backed by a low circular bank of stones and originally, a low cairn would have covered the interior of the circle. Ten pits were discovered within the circle during its excavation, with one pit lying near the centre and the others located near the edge, close to the uprights. Several of them featured cremation burials and the pit labelled 'Feature 8' contained a large and impressive Food Vessel of the Early Bronze Age into which the burnt remains of a young adult of indeterminate sex had been placed. It was clear that the pot had been decorated with a twisted cord when it was still wet, prior to its firing. Two holes drilled into the pot also revealed an unusual example of prehistoric repair, as with a string or cord pulled through them they would have helped pull together the bad crack that ran from the rim to the shoulder of the vessel. Such minor details may be of little importance, but they provide us with a little snapshot of human ingenuity that we ourselves can relate to. It is worth noting that this fine pot measures a substantial 0.32 metres in diameter and 0.35 metres tall.

Interestingly, two other pits contained cremations that were mixed with soils that had not come from the immediate area around Moel Goedog (they may have come from near Llanbedr or even Dyffryn Ardudwy a little further down

Food Vessel from Moel Goedog West with repair holes (redrawn after Lynch)

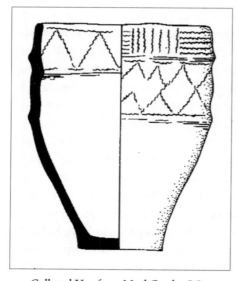

Collared Urn from Moel Goedog West

the coast). As Frances Lynch has noted, this indicates that small quantities of cremated bone or 'token burials' were brought to Moel Goedog 1 from other sites. In pit F. 10, a complete cremation burial of a young adult (again of unknown sex) was found in a fine Collared Urn of the Early Bronze Age. Pit F.7 produced another Collared Urn of good quality, but this larger pot contained only a mixture of dark earth and charcoal.

Moel Goedog East

This example of a Kerbed Cairn lies close to Moel Goedog West, slightly up the hill-slope to the north-east. Unfortunately, unlike its nearby partner it has not been excavated – at least not scientifically – and whether anything remains to be found at the site remains unknown. Moel Goedog East does not feature uprights and consists of a circular arrangement of large, squat boulders that are located on the inner edge of a low stony bank. It is evident that its central space was also levelled, no doubt to again facilitate the religious rituals and ceremonies that took place here. As with the stone circle pairs that we have already come across, we do not know which monument came first and whether separate groups were responsible for them.

However, future excavation may provide the answer to such questions.

Bedd Gorfal (Gorfal's grave)
Lying not far from the Moel Goedog circles, Bedd Gorfal is marked as a stone circle on the map, but it would perhaps be better to view this monument as the remains of a ring cairn because if it is an actual stone circle, it represents a very small example of one. Either way, there is no doubt that this peculiar little monument is located in an area that offers stunning views, with the mountain summits and heather-clad hills of western Snowdonia providing the visitor to the site with a superb panorama of north-Welsh countryside. As to the identity of Gorfal, this remains a mystery.

Other sites of interest
This area of Wales is very rich in prehistoric remains, but particularly notable is the superb and well known two-phase Neolithic tomb at Dyffryn Ardudwy where an earlier burial chamber was incorporated into a later long cairn (589228/124). The Coetan Arthur Neolithic tomb with its huge, toppled capstone is located just to the east of Dyffryn Ardudwy (603228/124). The remains of what must have been two impressive Neolithic tombs (labelled as *Carneddau Hengwm* on the map) can be seen near the Fridd Newydd circles. Close to these sites is Pen-y-Dinas, a small hillfort (607209/124) with an encircling stone wall that is quite well preserved. An unusual concentration of standing stones can be seen along the trackway leading to the Moel Goedog circles and it may be that these marked a ceremonial route that led to the circles. Finally, although I have not visited the site and I assume it will be quite hard to find, Cerrig-y-Cledd ('stone of the sword') must be mentioned. This large, natural boulder has split in two and

on each face of the separated stone there appear to be remarkable carvings of what look like the distinctive 'Carp's Tongue' swords used by Bronze Age warriors (see the *Megalithic Portal* for more on this highly intriguing site).

Chapter 5

Stone circles of northern Wales

The Penmaenmawr group

Y Meini Hirion/Druids' Circle

This circle has to be the finest example found in Wales and it would also be fair to count it among Britain's most notable prehistoric monuments. It seems safe to assume that this monument must have been of considerable importance when it was in use. The circle is located on the starkly beautiful upland that rises above the town of Penmaenmawr on the north Welsh coast and is just one of a number of stone circles and many other prehistoric monuments that can be found in this fascinating area. The Druids' Circle probably formed the central focus of an important religious sanctuary or 'cult centre' and people from both near and far probably came to perform rituals and ceremonies at the circle and the sites nearby.

The circle sits on the central plateau of the breezy, brown expanse of moorland known as Cefn Coch and lies next to an ancient trackway (now the popular North Wales Path) that runs up from the Llanfairfechan valley to cross the moorland and descend into the Conwy valley (or vice versa). From the circle, the views are truly magnificent, with the headland of Penmaenbach and the Great Orme (site of a remarkable Bronze copper mine) surrounded by wide expanses of sea and sky. To the south-west, the various peaks which mark this far northern edge of Snowdonia can be seen, while to the east, the hills of Foel Lwyd and Tal y

Fan dominate the horizon. About half a mile to the north-west is the great igneous outcrop of rock known as Graig Llwyd that protrudes from the eastern end of the headland of Penmaenmawr. Graig Llwyd marks the site of a modern quarry, but the remains of an important Neolithic axe factory were once located among its scarred and blasted slopes.

It is quite possible that the Druids' Circle was built around 3000 BC as it shares similarities with other stone circles of the Late Neolithic. If this was indeed the case, it could be that in its earliest phase, among other things, the Druid's circle functioned as a trading centre for stone axes from Graig Llwyd. Some support for this theory is perhaps provided by the fact that during the 1958 excavation of the site (directed by W. E. Griffiths) a 'rough-out' (an unfinished stone axe), the possible butt end of an axe and several flakes of stone were found, all of which derived from Graig Llywd. However, in the excavation report Griffiths says, 'I am inclined to believe that the presence of these pieces of worked Graig Llwyd rock is fortuitous and that they antedate the circle'.

Whether this is true cannot be proved, but it seems rather unlikely that these worked stones simply ended up here simply by chance and this writer feels it is more likely that they represent ritual depositions made within the circle. In the excavation report, Griffiths mentions that there are also stone axe factories to be found on the peaks of Foel Llwyd and Tal y Fan which lie about a mile away, and it could be that axes quarried from here also found their way into the hands of Late Neolithic people at the Druids' Circle. It will also be recalled from Chapter One that fragments of Graig Llwyd axes were found within Henge B at Llandegai. While this evidence does not prove that Late Neolithic people from the area around present-day Bangor where travelling to the Druids' Circle to obtain axes from Graig Llywd, it does indicate some form of contact between the two areas during this period. Mention should also be made of the fascinating evidence found in the early levels of the fascinating multi-phase ritual and burial site at Cairnapple Hill in West Lothian, which dates from c.2800–1500 BC. This evidence consisted of two fragments of stone axes – one from the axe factory at Great Langdale in the Lake District and one from Graig Llwyd. Whether Late Neolithic people from Scotland trekked to the Lake District and North Wales to obtain axes from these areas is debatable, but at the very least, as Ann MacSween has rightly said, 'it suggests that … the communities using Cairnapple were engaged in some form of trade with more distant groups'.

The Druids' Circle consists of some thirty stones of varying size, though originally there may have been more; as is often the way with stone circles and other prehistoric monuments, time (and people) have robbed us of a completely clear picture of what the Druids' Circle looked like when complete, but the site is still quite well preserved, nonetheless. The stones are set into a low, broad stony bank that is around 0.5 metres in height and which has a diameter of about 26 x 24.5 metres. In the south western side of the circle there is a gap measuring some 2.5 metres wide that marks the entrance into the interior of the monument. Griffiths' investigations revealed that the entrance had been badly ruined, but that originally, it was likely to have comprised of four portal stones, with two each flanking the entrance on either side. Portalled entrances are known at other stone circles, such as Long Meg and Her Daughters, and Swinside in the Lake District (the south-eastern entrance at Swinside faces the midwinter sunrise, while at Long Meg and Her Daughters, the entrance faces south-

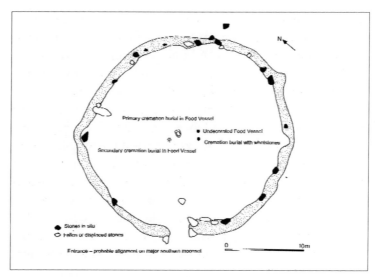

Plan of Druids' Circle (redrawn after Griffiths)

west towards a standing stone which probably marks the midwinter sunset) and as at these sites, the entrance at the Druids' Circle probably marks a celestial event, with two of the portal stones standing in line with the moon setting in its most southerly position. The long axis of the circle lies from south-east to north-west and Alexander Thom felt that this indicated the Beltane or May Day sunset.

Within the interior of the circle, a number of interesting discoveries were made and the first to be mentioned is the 'primary burial', which was found in a fine lozenge-shaped cist grave that lay near the centre of the circle. Inside the cist, a substantial, decorated Food Vessel was found that measured 12 inches high and which had a diameter of 10 inches. This pot contained the cremated remains of a child who was probably 10–12 years of age. About a metre from this burial a small pit was discovered and again, this contained a fairly large (around 9 inches in height and 8 inches in diameter) though undecorated Food Vessel, in which the cremated remains of another child (about 11–13 years old) had been placed. Also inside the pot was a small, bronze knife, which showed two rivet-holes for attachment to a handle. Eight feet south-east of the primary burial, the fragmentary remains

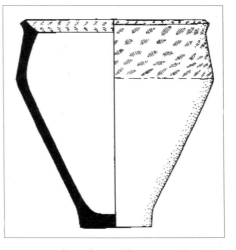

Decorated Food Vessel from Druids' circle (redrawn after Griffiths)

of another substantial and probably undecorated Food Vessel were found in a small pit. Although no traces of a cremation were associated with this pot, a shallow depression was also discovered next to it. This was lined with several small slabs of sandstone and upon these was laid the remains of another cremation burial, although because of the very poor condition of the bones nothing could be said in regard to the age or sex of the individual. Upon close examination of the stone slabs, they were found to be whetstones, with two showing clear signs that they had been used to sharpen a metal implement – probably a knife. If the Druids' Circle was indeed built around 3000 BC, the cremation burials show that many hundreds of years later, the monument was still being venerated as a sacred site, as Food Vessels are associated with the Early Bronze Age and date to *c.*2000–1500 BC. Also found during the excavation were many fragments of quartz of varying size that must have been transported to the site from elsewhere – though as Griffiths points out, they need not have come from any great distance as quartz can be found in the local erratics which litter the moorland. Nevertheless, the fact that quartz was transported to the site suggests that it had some sort of ritual significance to the builders of the Druids' Circle.

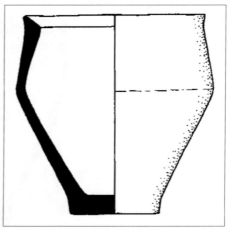

Undecorated Food Vessel from the Druids' Circle (redrawn after Griffiths)

We must also consider the possible implications of the evidence found within the Druids' Circle, as it may point to practices that to the modern mind at least, engender feelings of horror and revulsion. In the conclusion to the excavation report, Griffiths says in regard to the child cremation burials:

> [i]t seems inconceivable that so impressive a monument should have been raised merely to enshrine the ashes of children, however princely they may have been during their short lives. We cannot therefore entirely abandon the idea that such burials may have been dedicatory, and that the circular area defined by the bank and uprights, and hallowed by these burials, may have been used for ceremonial practices.

In other words, these burials may represent the burnt remains of children who were sacrificed on completion of the circle and buried in its interior as offerings to unknown prehistoric deities who, for some reason, demanded that their lives should be cut brutally short. Interestingly, in local folklore, stone 16, which has a natural ledge on its face, is said to have been used as an 'altar' on which sacrificed infants were placed during prehistoric ceremonies at the circle. It is likely that this folklore can be put down to an overactive and gruesome imagination, but child cremations are known at several other Neolithic and Bronze Age sites in Wales, and also elsewhere in Britain. There is a strong suspicion that at least some of these children were sacrificial victims who are likely to suffered terribly before their lifeless bodies were consigned to the flames of funeral pyres. Thus, while it seems very improbable that stone 16 was used as a sacrificial altar on which innocent babies were put to death, it is still not beyond the bounds of possibility that the Druids' Circle bore witness to the ritual murder of children on more than one occasion.

Circle No. 275

This interesting little monument is located some 300 metres north-east of the Druids' Circle, and like its more illustrious neighbour it is also located next to the ancient trackway that runs up from the lowlands. The monument is comprised of five rounded boulders which form a circle that measures about 4 metres in diameter. From its location, the Druids' Circle can clearly be seen to the south-west, its stones silhouetted against the skyline. Circle 275 was also excavated by W. E. Griffiths (in June 1959), and in comparison to his excavations at the Druids' Circle, his discoveries were somewhat disappointing. Nevertheless, he did find that many quartz fragments had been scattered

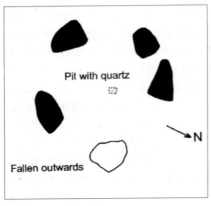

Pit with quartz

Fallen outwards

N

Plan of Circle 275
(redrawn after Griffiths)

inside the circle and that a dense mass of quartz fragments had also been placed in a small, shallow pit that had been dug near the centre of the circle. As we have seen above many quartz fragments were also found at the Druids' Circle and their appearance in both monuments lends strong support to the idea that quartz was in some way special to the prehistoric communities who deemed it worthy of inclusion in important religious sites. It could be that quartz was connected to religious ideas about the moon, which may perhaps have been viewed as a 'Land of the Dead', where the ancestors resided, or alternatively, it may have been seen as a powerful god or goddess. Again speculation rears its head with such ideas, but the probable lunar alignment at the Druids Circle and the fact that it is highly unlikely that prehistoric people viewed the moon from our detached 'western' perspective (although of course, like us they would surely have appreciated its beauty) suggest that they are worthy of consideration.

Although not particularly exciting in terms of actual finds, Circle 275 may provide fascinating evidence that it was Early Bronze Age people from across the Irish Sea who were responsible for its construction. As Aubrey Burl says of Circle 275:

the lowest but heaviest of the low boulders is at the south-west and this is the clue to its inspiration. It is a recognisable version of the Five-Stone recumbent stone circles of south-west Ireland [and] it may be assumed that its presence so far from its homeland was the result of traders in Irish copper ores bringing the material to north Wales and setting up their own small shrine.

This theory is open to question, but there can be no denying that it is an attractive and plausible one, nonetheless.

Circle No. 278

Located about 150 metres to the south-west of the Druids' Circle, this monument was also excavated by W. E. Griffiths in June 1959. It can be more correctly classified as a cairn circle rather than a freestanding stone circle, though as with Moel Goedog West, architectural quibbles should not overshadow the fascinating discoveries made here. The circle comprises of a low bank of stones (some 2.5 m in width) that measures around 12 metres in diameter and which appears to have been lined on its inner edge with a contiguous kerb of low stones. Although there appear to have been no stones that were of any significant size in this inner kerb, a fallen stone to the south-west (Stone F), would have measured just over one metre in height when upright, and there were was also a long, slab-like stone lying on its edge (Stone E, measuring about 1.5 m in length) on the south-east of the inner kerb. Griffiths felt that Stone E should be regarded as 'the foundation stone on which the whole circle was aligned', as it was associated with a cremation burial which was discovered under its eastern end, packed tightly into a small niche in the inner face of the bank. The cremated bones may have belon-ged to a woman;

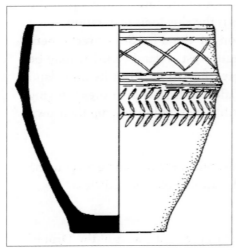

Collared Urn from Circle 278
(redrawn after Griffiths)

again, we are perhaps looking at the possibility that this individual was ritually killed as a dedicatory sacrifice on completion of the circle. It is also possible that Stone E was set up in line with the rising southerly moon.

Also found during the excavation was a small Collared Urn of the Early Bronze that had been placed in small, slab-covered pit which lay at exactly the opposite point in the circle to Stone E in an area of charcoal and blackened earth. Although no cremation burial was found within the urn, it did contain burnt earth and small amounts of unburnt soil and stone. From this mixture Griffiths reconstructed the likely sequence of events which had led to the deposition of the urn in the circle:

> A small circular pit was dug and a fire lit around and in it. When the fire died down, the ashes and blackened earth were scooped up together with soil and bits of gravel from the underlying surface, and with this material the urn was filled. The vessel was then placed mouth upwards in the hole; a slab of rock was dumped on top of it, cracking the urn as it fell into place; and a new fire was lit on top of the stone.

Monument 280

Exactly what this highly intriguing collection of large, jumbled stones (which lie just to the west of the Druids' Circle) represents is unclear, but it is generally thought that they are the remains of a cairn circle. However, it is not impossible that they mark the remains of an actual stone circle, although the former is probably more likely. Whatever the truth is behind these puzzling monoliths, it is very likely that they were erected by human hands thousands of years ago.

Red Farm

Only four stones of this monument survive, but it is evident that they belonged to an oval-shaped ring that measured around 25 by 21 metres in diameter. These remaining stones lie about half a mile to the east of the Druids' Circle and about 300 metres to the west of them, a massively squat, impressive 'playing-card' standing stone can be seen. It is quite possible that this massive stone is contemporary with the Red Farm circle, and interestingly it does appear to have been set up so that it faces towards the circle.

Hafodty

Although this circle is now in a somewhat ruinous condition, it would originally have been a fairly substantial monument. The circle has a diameter of around 11 metres and three stones remain standing, with three others lying prostrate. It is quite likely that three other stones have at some point been removed from the circle. One of the fallen stones measures about 1.5 metres in length; apparently this has been split by a dynamite blast. To the south-west of the site, Tal-y-Fan can be seen looming on the horizon and this distinctive peak may well have had been viewed as a sacred peak by the people who built this circle.

Cerrig Pryfaid

This strangely named circle of eleven or twelve low stones is located about two miles south of the Druids' Circle at the foot of Foel Lywd and sits on a flat spur of land that commands superb views out over rich farmland of the Conwy Valley to the east. To the north-west, the narrow pass known as Bwlch y Ddeufaen winds through the bare hills, where it exits at the low-lying coastal lands near the village of Llanfairfechan. As at several other stone circles in Wales, the May Day sunset may have been ritually important to the builders of Cerrig Pryfaid, as its long axis is aligned south-east to north-west, in line with an outlying stone that stands about 24 metres away.

Tyfos-Uchaf (possibly 'the house on the ditch')

This monument is located in some of the most delightful countryside in Wales and is found about 1.5 miles north-west of the pretty village of Llandrillo, in a field that overlooks the Dee. The monument consists of a ring of substantial boulders (around 17 metres in diameter) that appear to surround a low mound that probably represents the denuded remains of a burial cairn. The monument has therefore often been classified as ring cairn, but like Bryn Cader Faner (and other ring cairns), it could be a two-phase site and originally there may have a free-standing stone circle here, to which a burial cairn was added at a later date. It is also interesting to note that across the valley some 2 miles to the south-east, the false crest on which the cairn circle known as Moel-Tŷ-Uchaf is situated can clearly be seen. Although this monument cannot be seen today from Tyfos, it is quite possible that the cairn (which has long since disappeared) that originally covered the burial at Moel-Tŷ-Uchaf would have been visible from here when complete. Whether this was the case or not, standing at

Tyfos you are left with the distinct impression that there is a connection between the two monuments, particularly when it is considered that Tyfos can be seen down in the valley of the Dee, when you are standing high above it at Moel-Tŷ-Uchaf.

Moel-Tŷ-Uchaf ('the hill of Tŷ Uchaf')
This finely preserved and superb monument is one of Wales' most famous prehistoric sites and represents the remains of a cairn circle, though unfortunately no traces of the inner cairn now survive as it has long since been robbed away. Nevertheless, the forty-one boulders (all about 1.5 m high) that surrounded the cairn still survive to form an almost perfect circle that measures nearly 12 metres in diameter. The lack of a cairn means that a well-preserved cist-grave can clearly be seen in the centre of the circle. At

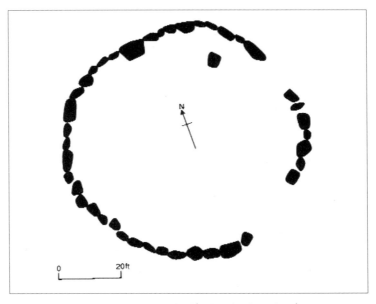

Plan of Moel-Tŷ-Uchaf (redrawn after Thom)

the south-south-west, there is a gap in the circle, which probably represents the original entrance into the interior. The site is situated on an outlier of the Berwyn Mountains and provides outstanding views of the rich agricultural land around Llandrillo. To the west the mountains which surround Llyn Celyn and Llyn Tegid (the lake near Bala) can be seen rising their distant heads, while to the east, hills of the Berwyn Range ring the circle. A short distance to the north-east, there is an outlying stone.

Rhos-y-Beddau ('moor of the graves')

Lying some 4.5 miles to the south of Moel-Tŷ-Uchaf, Rhos-y-Beddau is located above the stunning Pistyll Rhaeadr waterfall at the head of a long, steep valley. The monument consists of small stones that form a circle nearly 13 metres in diameter. A marked hollow in its centre probably marks the site of a former grave. Unfortunately, however, the stones of the circle are now hard to distinguish among the boggy vegetation that clothes the hillside. A double row or avenue of stones, which measures nearly 50 metres in length, leads to the circle from the east. As at Cerrig Duon, this avenue may have formed a ceremonial route for those approaching the circle to perform religious rites.

Penbedw Parc

This circle is situated in the splendid grounds of Penbedw Hall, which lies some five miles west of the town of Mold (*Yr Wyddgrug*) in Denbighshire. Today, only four stones remain, though there may originally have been ten or eleven stones standing in a perfect circle measuring 29.9 metres in diameter. Six stones are reputed to have been taken from the circle to be incorporated into farm buildings on the estate, and trees currently seen at the site are said to mark their former positions. There is, however, some question over the prehistoric authenticity of this monument circle: firstly, it stands very near to Penbedw Hall and secondly, it is also somewhat unusually situated on a slope. It is therefore quite possible that the circle may actually be a folly built by earlier occupants of the hall. However, in defence of its prehistoric pedigree, the circle does stand close to an important prehistoric route along which axes from Graig Llwyd were transported to the Peak District. Furthermore, there is also the fact that a Bronze Age burial mound can be seen about a quarter of a mile to the north-west of the circle. A low, but huge standing stone lies a couple of hundred metres to the south-west. Thus, taken together, the evidence suggests that is more likely that the circle is an original prehistoric construction rather than a much later one built on the whim of an aristocratic landowner.

Bryn Celli Ddu ('hill of the dark hazel grove')

Many people are likely to have visited the famous Neolithic

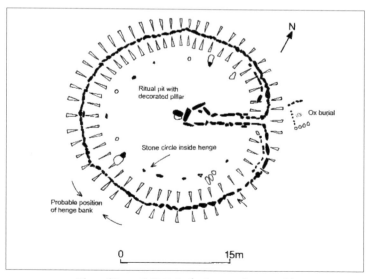

Plan of Bryn Celli Ddu (redrawn after Lynch)

Passage Grave of Bryn Celli Ddu, but not everybody may be aware that prior to the construction of this superb monument, a stone circle surrounded by a circular earthwork with an inner ditch (a henge) had stood here. There were probably originally sixteen standing stones that formed an oval measuring around 19 x 17 metres in diameter and the cremations of two young girls were buried within its interior. However, at some point in the Late Neolithic *c.*3000 BC the stone circle appears to have been destroyed, with some stones toppled and smashed, with others reused in the burial chamber. Bryn Celli Ddu represents a late example of a Passage Grave and was built around the same time that stone circles were becoming popular and chambered tombs were falling out of use. Therefore, many archaeologists have interpreted the architectural evidence at Bryn Celli Ddu as representing ideological conflict between two communities on Anglesey, with the destruction of the stone circle, and the subsequent building of the Passage Grave over it, representing one group's extreme refusal to accept the new tradition of stone circle building. If may even be that this conflict involved open warfare, although it must be pointed out that not all scholars agree with the suggested architectural sequence of events at Bryn Celli Ddu.

The tomb-builders made an intriguing deposit of a human earbone in a pit that had lain in the centre of the circle and covered this with a decorated slab that featured enigmatic carved decoration on its surfaces. An intriguing ox burial and the remains of a wooden structure were also found outside the entrance. Radiocarbon dating on decayed wood (pine) from the post-holes of the structure revealed that it had been set up in the Mesolithic period around 6000 BC. This evidence indicates that Bryn Celli Ddu was a sacred site long before Neolithic people came here and

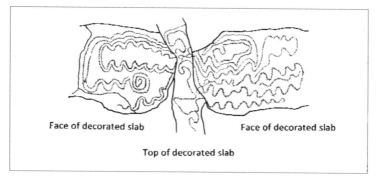

Face of decorated slab   Face of decorated slab

Top of decorated slab

Decorated Slab from Bryn Celli Ddu (redrawn after Lynch)

raised a Passage Grave for their dead – a pattern seen at other ritual and funerary monuments in Wales.

Bryn Gwyn ('white hill')
Not far from Bryn Celli Ddu near the late Neolithic earthwork known as Castell Bryn Gwyn (a possible fortified settlement) are two massive standing stones that reach some 3 and 4 metres high. It is likely that these impressive monoliths represent the sole survivors of a stone circle that was around 12 metres in diameter. If the lost stones were as large as the surviving ones, this must have been a very impressive and imposing monument in its original form.

The Llyn Brenig group

Like other monuments mentioned in this book, those of the Llyn Brenig group are not, strictly speaking, true stone circles (i.e. a freestanding ring of open and upright stones surrounding an open space). Nevertheless, like their counterparts, they could be said to belong to the stone circle 'family' and are impressive structures that have provided us with fascinating glimpses of the religious customs of the Early Bronze Age. Therefore, it again seems remiss not to include them within these pages.

The Llyn Brenig monuments are found on Mynydd Hiraethog, a wide area of moorland in Denbighshire, and lie in the upper reaches of the archaeologically-rich Brenig Valley, close to the broad expanse of the Llyn Brenig reservoir, which flooded a large part of the valley in the mid 1970s. They form part of an important Early Bronze Age religious complex (dating from c.2000–1500 BC) that features both funerary and ceremonial monuments (as well as the 'circles', several burial mounds are located in this area) that were excavated in 1973. It is evident that the Brenig Valley was an area of human activity long before people of the Early Bronze Age settled in this area, as evidence for a Mesolithic and Neolithic camp was also found during excavations of the prehistoric religious centre. It may also be interesting to note that in addition to this evidence for prehistoric activity, the remains of a post-medieval settlement (fifteenth to sixteenth century) comprising seven *hafodau* ('summer dwellings') and associated enclosures was also found. These rectangular, thatched stone houses were used as temporary summer bases by farmers who brought livestock into the rich grazing areas of the uplands during the kinder summer months.

Brenig 44
This fine Ring Cairn is located in a dominant position on a flat-topped promontory. It seems likely that this long-lived monument (which was probably in use for some 400 years) represents an important ceremonial centre within the Llyn Brenig religious complex. The first phase of the monument consisted of a low, well-constructed stone ring which featured several boulders of a considerable size in its inner

face. An unusual and fascinating additional feature of this first phase was the circle of free-standing posts that surrounded the cairn at a distance of about 2 metres. The holes that had held these posts (which had obviously long since rotted away – though modern replicas have replaced them) were carefully dug and their size suggests that substantial posts (about 1.5 m high) once stood in them. As Frances Lynch has said, 'It is tempting to imagine these posts elaborately carved like a series of protective totems around the sacred enclosure, rather than as a simple barrier or fence'. Around 100 years after the cairn and timber circle were constructed, the latter was removed and the stone ring was masked by the building of a sloping earth bank that completely covered its outer face. An incomplete bank was

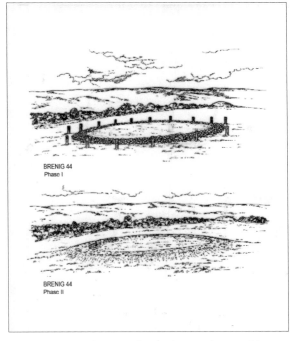

Brenig 44, Phase I and II (redrawn after Lynch)

built against the inner face of the stone ring in its earlier phase of use and the combination of the two banks radically transformed its appearance.

Four cremation burials were found within the interior of Brenig 44, though it was evident that these had been placed within the circle during the later phases of its history. Near the centre of the monument, a neatly-cut circular pit had been dug and the remains of a cremated adult were discovered just above a layer of reddish earth and oak charcoal that lay at its base. No artefacts were found with this burial. About 6 metres to the north-east of this burial, a large pit was found close to the foot of the inner wall of the stone ring. This pit contained an undecorated and decorated Collared Urn, with the former urn being of poorer quality than its decorated counterpart. The

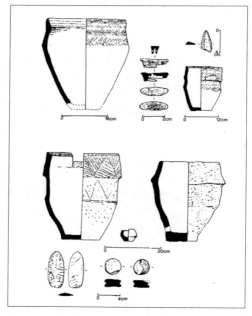

Grave goods from Brenig 44 (redrawn after Lynch)

undecorated urn held the cremated bones of a probable adult, while the latter contained the burnt remains of an adult and child; the child was probably about five years old when he or she was placed on a funeral pyre. A very small 'Accessory Cup', a fine flint knife and two pottery 'ear-studs' were found mixed with the burnt bones of the adult and child. As Frances Lynch has pointed out in regard to the term 'ear-studs', this is simply a convenient label and we are somewhat in the dark as to the true purpose of these small but intriguing items – though it is perhaps possible that they were used for fastening garments of some sort.

Brenig 51

This superb monument provides us with a highly impressive example of a Platform Cairn and lies about 0.5 miles south-east of Brenig 44. Although the cairn is located in a somewhat isolated and hidden position on the flat top of a ridge, it commands wide-ranging views of the surrounding landscape and also looks down and across to the other Llyn Brenig monuments. One is left with the impression that this marvellous example of Bronze Age religious architecture may well have been the most significant site for the people who came to 'worship' at the Llyn Brenig religious complex. The cairn is around 22 metres in diameter and consists of a wide, flat ring of large boulders, with a small circle of low standing stones on its inner edge and a kerb of massive boulders on its outer one. On the north-eastern side of the cairn, a small and curious Semi-Circle Cairn abuts the outer face of the kerb. Interestingly, a significant concentration of quartz was placed in the northern part of this cairn and the possible religious symbolism of quartz deposits has already been noted above at some of the Penmaenmawr monuments.

Although the size and location of Brenig 51 strongly

indicates that it was the most important site in the Brenig religious complex, it only yielded a small number of finds. As at Brenig 44, this suggests that the primary role of Brenig 51 had been ceremonial rather than funereal. Nevertheless, a small collared urn was found in the Semi-Circle Cairn and a Vase Urn containing the cremated remains of two adults was recovered from the main body of the Platform Cairn. Not far from this primary burial, to the north-east, the cremation of a child aged about eleven years old was discovered within the central area of the cairn, close to the inner edge of the small stone circle that defined the centre of the monument. A polished bone pommel from a bronze dagger was found with the two cremations in the Vase urn, and two flint knives were also discovered during the excavation of the site.

Brenig 8

Although not as impressive as its above neighbours, this monument nevertheless provides us with a fine example of a Kerbed Cairn. Brenig 8 is located a short way below Brenig 51 and as at the latter, the site commands wide-ranging views of the surrounding hills and distant mountains. The kerb of substantial boulders measures around 12 metres in diameter and although much of the cairn material had long since gone by the time the excavators came to the site to try to uncover its Bronze Age secrets, it was likely that the cairn had been quite high. Thus it would have been a conspicuous feature in the landscape that would have been clearly visible from afar.

A rectangular rock-cut pit was discovered by the excavators in the middle of the cairn and this contained a small and fragmentary deposit of burnt human bone, perhaps representing the burial of a child. No grave goods were found with the cremation burial, but a number of finds

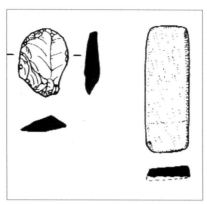

*Scraper and whetstone from Brenig 8
(redrawn after Lynch)*

were recovered from the topsoil: a whetstone and both Bronze Age and Mesolithic flints, with the latter indicating hunter-gatherer activity on the ridge. Included among the Bronze Age flints was a high quality scraper. The remains of a post-medieval longhouse or *hafod* (Hen Ddinbych) are also clearly visible in the valley just below the site.

Other sites of interest

As mentioned above, the area around Penamaenmawr has a very rich concentration of prehistoric remains and a number of Neolithic tombs can be seen in the area with Maen-y-Bardd providing a well known example (740717/115). Not far from the Druids' Circle is Graig Llywd Neolithic axe factory (717749/115), though I am unsure what remains of this fascinating site, as I have not visited it and modern quarrying still takes place nearby. Also of note in this area is the cairn cemetery that lies about 0.5 miles west from the Druids' Circle. There are also many fine prehistoric monuments to be seen in Denbighshire, though the most remarkable has to be the hugely enigmatic Gop Cairn or Cop y Goleuni ('mount of lights' – after its use as a beacon in the seventeenth century) not far from Prestatyn (086802/116). This huge, man-made oval mound, which measures some 300 by 250 feet and around 8 metres high, dates to the Neolithic period, though like its larger counterpart of Silbury Hill in Wiltshire, its true purpose is frustratingly unknown. The site was excavated in the late nineteenth century, but results were disappointing with no evidence found to show that the Gop was a huge burial chamber as has been suggested by some. Just to the south of Gop Cairn are the fascinating Gop Caves (086801/116), where excavations in the nineteenth century revealed that at least fourteen people had been buried here during the Neolithic and that the caves had also been used by a pack of hyenas during the last Ice Age. The fine chain of hillforts that run along the beautiful hills of the Clwydian Range (e.g. Moel-y-Gaer, Moel Arthur and Pen-y-Cloddiau) also have to be included in this brief list.

Gazetteer

The numbers in brackets after site names refer to grid references and corresponding maps. In terms of weather conditions, the best time to visit the circles is obviously the summertime. However, in terms of the actual visibility of several of the circles, it is during the winter, when the vegetation has died back, that you will get your best view of them. If you are planning to visit sites, take a compass and a mobile phone if striking out on your own. Many of the circles are located in upland areas, there is often boggy or wet ground to contend with even in the summer months, and so I recommend a good pair of walking boots (preferably completely waterproof!). Please respect the Country Code (see page 13), and private property.

Stone circles of south-western Wales

Gors Fawr (134293/145)
Take the minor road from the village of Mynachlog-ddu for about 1 mile and follow the footpath on the right of the road to the circle, which can easily be seen on the common.

Bedd Arthur (131324/145)
From the car-park at the bottom of Mynydd Bach follow the footpath to the top of the hill, bear right and follow the trackway for about 1 mile (making sure you pass the outcrops of Carn Sian and Carn Bica) and keep walking until you come across Bedd Arthur just to the left.

Dyffryn Syfynwy (059284/145)
From Mynachlog-ddu follow the B4313 towards Fishguard (*Abergwaun*) for about 7 miles. The circle lies south of

Rosebush Reservoir and is reached by walking to the end of the track that leads to Dyffryn farm and then by bearing sharply west for about 230 metres.

Meini Gwŷr/Buarth Arthur (142267/145)
To reach this monument, simply follow the minor road that leads left from the pub at Glandy Cross (do not take the road that leads uphill to Mynachlog-ddu) and you will soon come to Meini Gwŷr, which is signposted.

Stone circles of central and southern Wales

Eglwys Gwyddelod (663002/135)
The shortest way to reach this site is by following the footpath from near Caeceinach farm. However, I followed the lane up from near Rhyd-yr-Onen station (on the delightful Talyllyn railway) that climbs up a beautiful, secluded river valley (Nant-braich-y-Rhiw) to link up with a footpath that takes you to the site. When you come to the end of the lane, follow the path upwards until you come to a post marking three footpaths and take the left-hand path down for about 1.5 miles until you come to a metal gate. The circle lies just to the left of this gate, on a spur. The going is fairly arduous, but it is well worth the effort as you will get to see some glorious countryside along the way.

Ysbyty Cynfyn (752791/135)
This disputed but probable prehistoric circle is easily reached by following the A4120 from Devil's Bridge for about 2 miles. You will see the church set just off the road to the left.

Cerrig Gaerau and Lled-Croen-yr-Ych (903005/136)

Visiting these circles requires a fair level of fitness (the same can be said for many other sites included in this book!) as they are located at the top of a steep footpath that leads up on to the summit of Newydd Fynyddog. From Talerdigg, follow the A470 for about 2 miles until near Werngerhynt you see will see a footpath sign on the left, pointing to a gate on the right. Go through this gate and then another, and follow the footpath uphill until you come to the circles. Lled-Croen-Yr-Ych lies about 100 metres to the north-east of Cerrig Gaerau.

Ceri Hill (158860/136)

Follow A489 from Newtown to Ceri and continue on B4368, taking the (steep) minor road just before Block Wood. At the top of Ceri Hill you will see the famous 'Ceri Pole' with its fox sitting on top. The footpath to the circles lies just before this to the right. Go through two gates and take the track branching left off the Ridgeway. Walk for a short way down this until you see three telegraph poles to your right. Bear to the right of the middle pole and keep walking until you come to the circle.

Y Capel (999000/136)

The easiest way to reach this circle appears to be to follow the minor road that bears right off the A483 just after Carno. Follow the road for about 4 miles and take the footpath or track that leads to Esgair Cwmowen. The circle lies in between the footpath and track, although as I have not visited the site it is hard to be sure about the exact nature of the local terrain.

Trecastle Mountain (833311/160)

Follow A4069 through Llandovery and take the first right

after the castle. Follow the minor road until it ends near Hafod Fawr farm. Follow the footpath up on to the moorland and walk for about 1.5 miles until you come to the denuded earthworks of the Roman marching camps. Walk past these, until in the distance you can see a forestry plantation on hills to your left. Head across the moorland towards these hills and keep walking until you come to the circles.

Cerrig Duon (851206/160)

Take minor road that leads through Bwlch Cerrig Duon ('Cerrig Duon pass') and links Trecastle with Glyntawe. About 2 miles after Glasfyndd Forest you will start to descend – look right and you will see Cerrig Duon and Maen Mawr (though the latter monument will be more readily apparent) above the Tawe. To reach the site you have to cross the Tawe, but it is not particularly wide and deep and so presents no real problems for would-be visitors. However, take care of slippery rocks!

Nant Tarw (820258/160)

Follow the minor road that leads west out of Trecastle until you come to Blaenau Uchaf Farm. From here, follow the footpath west for about 1 mile, crossing Nant Tarw brook in the process, and you will come to the circles.

Ynys Hir (921383/160)

As mentioned above, this circle is situated on Ministry of Defence land and permission in writing is needed by people wishing to visit the site. Those readers who would like to visit the circle should contact: Sennybridge Training Area, near Brecon, Powys, LD3 8PN. The Ministry of Defence has helpfully provided tall posts which mark the locations of the circle and nearby cairn.

Four Stones (245607/137)

From New Radnor (*Maesyfed*) follow the A44 towards Kington for about 2.5 miles and take the first left after Downton. Follow this lane for about 1 mile until you see a footpath sign on the right – the Four Stones lie in the field opposite, just next to the hedge.

Llorfa (786155/160)

Follow the bridleway north-west from near Tu-hwnt farm for about 2 miles until it splits in two. Follow the right-hand track for about 1 mile and you should see the circle to one side or the other, though its stones will probably not be easily visible amongst the thick moorland vegetation.

Crugiau Bach (931624/147)

This circle is located above the village of Llanwrthwl, near Llandrindod Wells, but I am not sure how one reaches it.

Stone circles of north-western Wales

Cerrig Arthur (631188/124)

From Barmouth town centre head towards Barmouth Bridge, take first left after the Museum and follow the steep lane (Panorama Road) for about 2 miles to its end near Sylfaen farm. Walk through the farmyard and go through the gate on left, following the grassy footpath for a short way until you come to the circle.

Ffridd Newydd (616213/124)

Take the straight lane that leads up to Meifod Uchaf farm from the A496 just before Dyffryn Ardudwy. Bear right following the footpath over the Ysgethin and walk for about a mile. The circles lie in a field, just to the right of the path.

Bryn Cader Faner (648353/124)

From the lovely hamlet of Eisingrug take the very steep lane that leads up behind the hotel and follow for about 1 mile until you come to a gate and the footpath that will take you to the site. Follow the footpath until it splits in two, then follow the left-hand track for about a mile and you will clearly see the circle sitting on its spur of land at the head of the valley.

Llyn Eidew Bach (646349/124)

This circle lies just to the right of the track that leads to Bryn Cader Faner and is located about 0.5 miles from this fine monument. Look out also, for the ring cairns that are located nearby and the fine hut-circles (probably Iron Age in date).

Moel Goedog West & East (610324/124)

From the centre of Harlech take the steep road that climbs up to the crossroads near the phone-box. Take the left-hand lane and follow for about 1.5 miles until it joins up with the footpath that will lead you in a short while to the circles. (You will know you are getting close to the site when you see the first of the standing stones that may have marked a ceremonial route to the Moel Goedog circles.)

Bedd Gorfal (612311/124)

This circle can be visited in conjunction with a trip to the above monuments and is easily reached by taking the lane that bears right after the first standing stone on the above 'ceremonial route' to Moel Goedog. Follow for about 0.5 miles until you come to a footpath on your left and follow this for a short way to the circle, which is set a little way back off the footpath.

Stone circles of northern Wales

Druids' Circle (723746/115)
From the centre of Penmaenmawr follow signs for the 'Jubilee Footpath' up Fernbrook Road and take first right at Merton Park Road. Keep following the road up, until you come to a sign for 'Graig Llwyd Springs' fishing ponds. Follow the footpath past the ponds and cross the fields until you link up with the lane that leads you to a footpath (you will see a sign for Snowdonia National Park) which climbs steeply up to the signposted track (the North Wales Path) that takes you to the Druids' Circle. When you come to a pleasant section of the track that is lined by pine trees, look out for the huge 'playing-card' standing stone (you cannot miss it!) just to the left of the solitary house below Craig Hafodwen. After this section of the track, bear right through the gate and you are on your way to the Druids' Circle and the sites immediately below.

Circle 275, 278 and monument 280 (115)
These sites lie very close to the Druids' Circle and are easily found. For more specific locations see Chapter 5.

Red Farm (732750/115)
The remains of this circle are situated in a field a couple of hundred yards north-east of the 'playing-card' standing stone mentioned above.

Hafodty (747752/115)
From the Druids' Circle head back towards Penmaenmawr on North Wales Path, passing the playing-card standing stone and Red Farm circle. Bear right before Craig Hafodwen, walk for about a mile and then take the right-hand path that leads to the circle.

Cerrig Pryfaid (724713/115)
This circle is situated some 2 miles north of the Druids' Circle and is located in a field just next to the narrow lane that leads to the car-park at the foot of Foel Lwyd (note that this area provides the prehistoric enthusiast with much of interest).

Tyfos-Uchaf (028388/125)
From Llandrillo take the road (B4401) west across the Afon Drfrdwy (Dee), turn right and after about a mile you will come to Tyfos farm on the left – the circle lies in a field just in front of the house and its large stones can be easily be seen.

Moel-Tŷ-Uchaf (057371/125)
The easiest way to reach this site is to follow the B4401 north for about a mile until you come to a phone box. Take the first right immediately after the phone box and follow the steep lane and mountain track to the circle, which sits on a spur of land just to the left of the track.

Rhos-y-Beddau (058302/125)
From Tan-y-pistyll, follow steep footpath that climbs above Pistyll Rhaiddar waterfall and bear north-west for about a mile up the steep-sided and narrow valley, at the head of which, the circle stands.

Penbedw Parc (171679/116)
Follow the A541 from Mold towards Denbigh (*Dinbych*) and after about 8 miles you will see a gatehouse that stands just to the left of the road in the grounds of Penbedw Hall. The circle lies in a field that can be reached by following the track that runs just to the side of the gatehouse.

Bryn Celli Ddu (507702/115)

This superb monument lies some 3 miles south-west of the Menai Bridge and about 1 mile east of Llanddaniel-fab. It is signposted and easily reached.

Bryn Gwyn (463669/115)

From above, continue along the A4080 past Bryn Gwyn Hall and after a couple of hundred metres you will see a footpath sign on the right. Cross the stile and follow the hedge on the right for some 300 metres and you will come to the two impressive standing stones that are all that remain of this former circle.

Llyn Brenig Group (Brenig 44: 983572, Brenig 8: 987564, Brenig 51: 989566/116)

These monuments are easily reached by following the archaeological trail that starts at the northern end of the reservoir (a useful guide to the trail can be purchased from the visitor centre at the southern end of Llyn Brenig). Go through the gate, follow the trail, and you will soon come to Brenig 44 on the right, near the water's edge (a Bronze Age burial mound is also clearly visible close to the Ring Cairn and you will see this first). From here, walk along the trail for a short way and you will see a deserted farmhouse – follow the trail past this and bear right up the rutted track to the top of the hill. Keep bearing right and follow the two signposts that lead the way to the Kerbed Cairn. To reach Brenig 51, simply walk uphill to the north-east for about 400 metres from Brenig 8 and you will find this hugely impressive monument on top of the ridge.

Glossary of terms

AOC (All-Over-Cord) Beaker: Distinctive pots associated with the first continental immigrants (probably from the Low Countries) of the famous Beaker Culture who arrived in Britain about 2500 BC. Decorated with twisted cords or animal gut – some archaeologists also believe that twisted cords of cannabis hemp were used to decorate them.

Barbed and Tanged Arrowheads: Again, introduced into Britain by members of the Beaker Culture and probably designed primarily as weapons of war.

Bronze Age (*c.*2200–800 BC): The period in which bronze metalwork came into use. It appears to have been a very warlike time, as large numbers of bronze weapons and fortified settlements survive from this time. It is evident that many Iron Age hillforts actually originated in the later Bronze Age.

Cist Grave: Large stones usually set in rectangular arrangements to form graves.

Collared Urn: Type of Early Bronze Age funerary vessel in which cremations were placed.

Copper Age (*c.*2500–2200 BC): The short-lived but highly significant period in which metalworking (and the mining of copper and gold), new ideologies, practices and fashions were introduced into Britain by people of the Beaker Culture.

Embanked Stone Circle: Stone circles (roughly dating

from 2900–2200 BC) featuring a low bank of earth or stones (or a combination of the two) in which stones were set.

Food Vessel: Again, funerary vessels of the Early Bronze Age which contained cremations.

Four Poster: Small 'circles' which actually consist of four stones forming a rectangle. They date to *c.*2200–1500 BC and are mainly confined to north-east Scotland.

Henge: Earthwork monuments that were built from *c.*3200–2000 BC. Archaeological evidence found within them suggests that they were primarily ritual and ceremonial monuments.

Neolithic (*c.*4000–2500 BC): The highly important period in which the hunting and gathering, semi-permanent lifestyle of the Mesolithic (*c.*8000–4000 BC) was replaced by one based on a farming economy and permanent settlements. Archaeological evidence has revealed that this period was also far from peaceful and that warfare was not unknown.

Passage Grave: Neolothic funerary monuments featuring passages that lead into inner burial chambers and which are sometimes decorated with highly enigmatic abstract 'art'.

Platform Cairn: Monuments (primarily ceremonial) constructed during the Early Bronze Age and that basically consist of low platforms of earth or stone surrounded by a circular ring of large stones or boulders.

Accessory/Pygmy Cup: Small pottery vessels made during

the Early Bronze Age. Their true purpose is unclear, but some archaeologists have suggested that they may have been used as narcotic burners.

Useful Websites

The Megalithic Portal: A superb website that is packed full of useful information on prehistoric sites in Britain and elsewhere, in Europe and beyond.

Coflein: The excellent website of the Royal Commission on Ancient and Historical Monuments in Wales, which, amongst other things, contains photographs and distribution maps of prehistoric and later sites.

Megalithic Walks: This fine website is run by two megalithic 'devotees' – Graham and Angela Tickner. It lists many megalithic sites throughout Britain, and along with many photographs of these sites it also provides very useful information on how to reach them.

Aenigmatis: Martin. J. Powell's interesting website, which also includes a section on Welsh stone circles and the fascinating subject of Archaeoastronomy.

The Modern Antiquarian: Another good website (based on Julian Cope's bestselling book of the same name) that provides much information on British and European prehistoric sites.

Landscape Perception: A well-presented website that looks at landscape and acoustic aspects of prehistoric sites, with Carn Menyn as its pilot study.

Select Bibliography

Banks, R. W., 'The Four Stones, Old Radnor', in *Archaeologia Cambrensis* V, 215–217 (1874)

Bradley, R., *The Significance of Monuments: On the shaping of human experience in Neolithic and Bronze Age Europe* (Routledge, 1998)

Briggs, C. S., 'Ysbyty Cynfyn Churchyard Wall', in *Archaeologia Cambrensis* CXXVIII, 138–147 (1978)

Burl, A., *The Stone Circles of the British Isles* (Yale University Press, 1976)

Burl, A., 'Science or Symbolism: problems of archaeo-astronomy', in *Antiquity* 54, 191–201 (1980)

Burl, A., *Rites of the Gods* (J. M. Dent and Sons, 1981)

Burl., A., *Four-Posters: Bronze Age Stone Circles of Western Europe* (British Archaeological Reports 195, 1988)

Burl, A., *Prehistoric Astronomy and Ritual* (Shire, 1997)

Burl, A., *Circles of Stone: The Prehistoric Rings of Britain and Ireland* (Harvill Press, 1999)

Burl, A., *Prehistoric Stone Circles* (Shire, 2005)

Burl, A., *A Brief History of Stonehenge* (Robinson, 2007)

Burton, P., 'Megalithic Magnetism', in *3rd Stone*, 42–53 (2003)

Bushell, Rev. W. D., 'Amongst the Prescelly Circles', in *Archaeologia Cambrensis* XI, 287–334 (1911)

Butler, F. and Butler, J., 'Y Capel: A Stone Circle near Cefn Coch, Llanllugan', in *Archaeologia Cambrensis* CXXVII, 122–124 (1978)

Catling, C., 'Message in the Stones', in *Current Archaeology* 212, 12-20 (2007)

Catling, C., 'Bluestonehenge', in *Current Archaeology* 237, 22–29 (2009)

Crawford, O. G. S., 'Account of Excavations at Hengwm, Merionethshire, August and September, 1919', in *Archaeologia Cambrensis* XX, 99–134 (1920)

Cummings, V. and Whittle, A., *Places of Special Virtue: Megaliths in the Neolithic Landscapes of Wales* (Oxbow 2004)

Darvill, T. and Wainwright, G., 'SPACES – exploring Neolithic landscapes in the Strumble-Preseli area of southwest Wales', in *Antiquity* 76, 263–264 (2002)

Darvill, T. and Wainwright, G., 'Stone Circles, Oval Settings and Henges in South-West Wales and Beyond', in *The Antiquaries Journal* 83, 9–47 (2003)

Dunning, G. C., 'A Stone Circle and Cairn on Mynydd Epynt, Brecknockshire', in *Archaeologia Cambrensis*, XCVII, 169–195 (1943)

Fitzpatrick, A., 'The Boscombe Bowmen: Builders of

Stonehenge?', in *Current Archaeology* 193, 10–16 (2004)

Gibson, A. and Simpson, D., (eds), *Prehistoric Ritual and Religion: Essays in Honour of Aubrey Burl* (Sutton, 1998)

Griffiths, W. E., 'The Excavation of Stone Circles near Penmaenmawr, North Wales', in *Proceedings of the Prehistoric Society* XXVI, 303–340 (1960)

Hadingham, E., *Early Man and the Cosmos* (Heinemann, 1983)

Hawkes, J., 'God in the Machine', in *Antiquity* XLI, 174–180 (1967)

Hawkins, G. S., *Stonehenge Decoded* (Doubleday, 1965)

Houlder, C. H., 'The Henge Monuments at Llandegai', in *Antiquity* 42, 216–221 (1968)

Hoyle, J. R., 'A Survey of some of the Stone Rings of Mid Wales', in *Archaeologia Cambrensis* CXXIII, 51–64 (1984)

Jones, N. W., 'Crugiau Bach and Llorfa stone circles, Brecknock', in *Archaeologia Cambrensis* 156 (2007)

Lynch, F., *Prehistoric Anglesey* (Anglesey Antiquarian Society, 1970)

Lynch, F., 'Moel Goedog 1: a Complex ring Cairn near Harlech', in *Archaeologia Cambrensis* CXXXIII, 8–51 (1984)

Lynch, F., *Excavations in the Brenig Valley: A Mesolithic and*

Bronze Age Landscape in North Wales (Cambrian Archaeological Monographs No. 5, 1993)

Lynch, F., Aldhouse-Green, S. and Davies J. L., *Prehistoric Wales* (Sutton, 2000)

Mackie, E. W., 'Wise Men in Antiquity?', in Ruggles, C. and Whittle, A (eds) *Astronomy and Society in Britain during the Period 4000–1500 BC* (British Archaeological Reports 88, 1981).

Marshall, P., *Europe's Lost Civilization: Exploring the Mysteries of the Megaliths* (Headline, 2004)

Michell, J., *A Little History of Astro-Archaeology* (Thames & Hudson, 1989)

Mohen, J-P., *Standing Stones: Stonehenge, Carnac and the World of the Megaliths* (Thames and Hudson, 1999)

Parker Pearson, M. & Ramilisonina, 'Stonehenge for the ancestors: the stones pass on the message', in *Antiquity* 72 (1998)

Parker Pearson, M., Chamberlain, A., Jay, M., Marshall, P., Pollard, J., Richards, C., Thomas, J., Tilley, C. and Welham, K., 'Who was buried at Stonehenge?', in *Antiquity* 83, 23–39 (2009)

Parker Pearson, M., Pollard, J. and Welham, K., 'Newhenge', in *British Archaeology* 110, 14–22 (2010)

Peat, I. C., 'The Gorsedd of the Bards of Britain', in *Antiquity* 25, 13–15 (1951)

Piggot, S., 'The Sources of Geoffrey of Monmouth', in *Antiquity* 60, 305–319 (1941)

Pryor, F., *Britain BC: Life in Britain and Ireland before the Romans* (Harper Collins, 2003)

Ruggles, C., *Astronomy in Prehistoric Britain and Ireland* (Yale University Press, 1999)

Ruggles, C., *Ancient Astronomy: An Encyclopedia of Cosmology and Myth* (ABC-CLIO, 2005)

Thom, A., *Megalithic Sites in Britain* (Oxford University Press, 1967)

Thom, A., *Megalithic Lunar Observatories* (Oxford University Press, 1971)

Thom, A., and Thom, A. S., 'Megalithic Rings: Collated with archaeological notes', by A. Burl (*British Archaeological Reports* 81, 1980)

Wood, J. E., *Sun, Moon and Standing Stones* (Oxford University Press, 1978)